LOOKING BACK TO MOVE FORWARD

Exposing Our Cultural Taboos
Whilst Keeping Traditions Alive

LILLIAN MUCHIRI

First published by Ultimate World Publishing 2023
Copyright © 2023 Lillian Muchiri

ISBN

Paperback: 978-1-922828-93-4
Ebook: 978-1-922828-94-1

Lillian Muchiri acknowledges that this book contains traditional medical procedures and warns the reader that some contents may be confronting. The information contained in this book is based on the author's experiences and opinions.

The moral right for Lillian Muchiri to be identified as the author of this work has been asserted in accordance with the Copyright, Designs and Patents ACT of 1998. The publisher specifically disclaims responsibility of any adverse consequences which may arise from use of the information contained herein. Permission to use information has been sought by the author. Any breaches will be rectified in further editions of this book.

All rights reserved. No part of this publication may be reproduced, stored in or introduced into a retrieval system, or transmitted in any form, or by any means (electronic, mechanical, photocopying, recording or otherwise) without the prior written permission of the copyright owner and the publisher of this book.

Any person who does any unauthorised act in relation to this publication may be liable to criminal prosecution and civil claims for damages.

Cover design: Ultimate World Publishing
Layout and typesetting: Ultimate World Publishing
Editor: Alex Floyd-Douglass

Cover picture description: Mum holding me as an infant, dad and a refurbished house we grew up in.

Ultimate World Publishing
Diamond Creek,
Victoria Australia 3089
www.writeabook.com.au

TESTIMONIALS

"*Lillian writes with a directness that brings you straight to the heart of the matter. An important story that needs to be shared.*"
- Zindzi Okenyo (Australian musician and actress)

"*What an incredible book. I am so glad someone was brave enough to shed this light on the world. It's vulnerable and raw.*" - Natalie

"*I would recommend this book to anyone looking for inspiration and motivation.*" - Kate

"*Wow! What heavy subjects and so courageous of you to share your stories.*" - Lisa

"*This book is sensational, I couldn't stop venturing into it, so educational.*" - Helen

"*Good on you for sharing your story, this is for everyone.*" - Maggy

"*Oh, my goodness, this is some great content.*" - Jeremy

"*Hell no, don't stop writing, put it out there.*" - Joey

"*Thank you for telling it out for all of us.*" - Maureen

"*This book will shake you to the core.*" - Abby

"*I absolutely loved it.*" - Tiffany

"*Phenomenal.*" - Mark

MY RESPECT

In this book, I wish to acknowledge the land that I live in. I pay my respect to the original custodians of Australian land, the elders that have passed, and those present living with us.

I wish to thank you for allowing people from all walks of life to come and live here, to find solace and comfort.

I wish to acknowledge the peace and prosperity of the Australian country in present times and embrace the culture that is shared and ongoing awareness about sharing their resources with anyone who calls Australia home.

Thank you to the Australian lawmakers and keepers who continue to serve the country to ensure that we are all safe.

DEDICATION

To Oliver and Jabari, you are my warriors; the sky is your limit.

To Mum, Dad and my siblings, look how far we have come and where we are today; let's keep *Looking Back to Move Forward*.

In my long journey, I found great genuine friends. If you have influenced me positively, let us maintain the momentum.

To my readers, we cannot change a past that we have not experienced and disliked. I appreciate you. This book is for you.

To the almighty God, thank you for your mercies are forever, you promised that you will never fail, and you haven't.

CONTENTS

Testimonials	iii
My Respect	v
Dedication	vii
The Project Inspired by this Book	xi
Introduction	1
Chapter One: Disparities and Experiences	3
Chapter Two: My Philosophy in Life	17
Chapter Three: Growing Up	23
Chapter Four: Mum	39
Chapter Five: Dad	49
Chapter Six: Michael	57
Chapter Seven: Primary School	63
Chapter Eight: Secondary School	69
Chapter Nine: National Youth Service	77
Chapter Ten: Paramilitary Training	85
Chapter Eleven: Women	95
Chapter Twelve: Adult Life and Migration from Kenya	113

LOOKING BACK TO MOVE FORWARD

Chapter Thirteen: University	121
Chapter Fourteen: My Boys	129
Chapter Fifteen: Racism	137
Chapter Sixteen: Reflection	143
References	151
Information About Karibu Women's and Children's Home	153
About the Author	155
Speaker Bio	157
Acknowledgements	159

THE PROJECT INSPIRED BY THIS BOOK

Looking Back to Move Forward may mean something different to each person depending on what they want to shine a light on, or grow from and move forward. My book was written inspired by events of my childhood, upbringing, schooling, work and life in Kenya as a young adult – and life after migration to Australia.

Due to the hardships, I saw children and women go through, I vowed to my mum and myself that one day I would take up a cause to challenge these customs and unjust practices and deliver change and hope for Kenyan women.

Sometimes change needs to happen, but unless someone talks and starts something to help the community, people may not know about such issues and change may never start.

LOOKING BACK TO MOVE FORWARD

Twenty years ago, I started a conversation with Mum about the inequalities she faced and how she felt as a girl and later, a woman growing up. I did not know where to start.

Mum smiled and said, *"Kagendo, these things are heavy in my heart, but I do not know what we can do to help change."*

My sister Florence – who is still a very beautiful woman and a kind, generous and qualified teacher – has been very inspiring. She has gone through a similar experience in a way. She had to look after all of us when we were growing up. Although her back problems have almost crippled her, she has not given up her job as a teacher.

Over time, I bought land in Kenya, located in my village for the women's shelter, but it has not been that simple to plan and build, the timing was not right. I believe the time has come for this initiative to kickstart.

Once completed, the women's shelter will be run by local women to provide some purpose and impact in the community. Girls will be empowered, they will have something they resonate with, role models in the community, someone to counsel and inspire them to reach their dreams and a changed community perspective from what has been engrained for centuries.

I feel that time has passed when things should have started, and I am excited to finally unveil this concept I have had since my teenage years.

My mum is a great cook and very good at nurturing people. Although she won't be with us for long, she has done her part in raising us. We have a community of resilience; a tough upbringing that lacked growth and opportunity because there was no one

THE PROJECT INSPIRED BY THIS BOOK

available to start something substantial to give back to people to reach their potential.

I am very privileged to be born into this era, where I can look back on decades of pure turmoil yet see the potential for a shift. My early life experiences did not break me but instead, they made me brave and insightful – and taught me resilience; to never give up.

I have also had interactions with children of this generation in Australia and how they view the world through their lens. Compared to what my experiences were and still are going on in my village, most children have been left in awe when they hear the stories and would do anything to help their counterparts. They have expressed the need to pass the awareness of my upbringing to theirs.

With big support from my mum, sisters, and our community, we will start a change, however small, and we won't stop – however long it will take.

INTRODUCTION

Thank you, my readers; you are the reason I wrote this book. To show you all that nothing is easy out in the village and in this world, but we can embrace experiences to give us grit and perseverance.

To help our friends that are struggling because life is meant to be enjoyed, I find no use seeing another person struggling and turning a blind eye. Kindness is free to give and receive – let us exchange it.

To all the children in my village and in other parts of the world who sleep and go to school hungry, brush their teeth with tree twigs, walk everywhere barefoot in scorching heat and on prickles, and have no role models to guide their way. No matter where you are at present, what your experiences are, they do not define you. Try your best, keep your head up, and do not give up.

To the many beautiful children in the Western world, free from war and able to receive utmost health care, appreciate what you have, and work with your parents and teachers to help achieve your dreams. You are very protected, loved and privileged

LOOKING BACK TO MOVE FORWARD

– make use of these opportunities and do not take these things for granted.

To all the beautiful and tough women in the world who have influenced change; those of colour or not; those who have or may not have walked my path; those going through tough times. We are sisters; a big ocean; we do not run dry. We hold the world together; we do not give up. We are on the move.

We support each other in difficult times, and we will live to enjoy a truer, more authentic and more beautiful life, free from pain. Just remember that we are living in the future that our ancestors once talked about.

We are the change, so let us support each other in achieving the unknown.

Lastly, to all the men in the world, support the women in your life so they can help you build your family and make the world a better place. Let us all invest in children, girls and women, because by doing so, we are investing in the world by uplifting humankind.

Love and light.

Chapter One

DISPARITIES AND EXPERIENCES

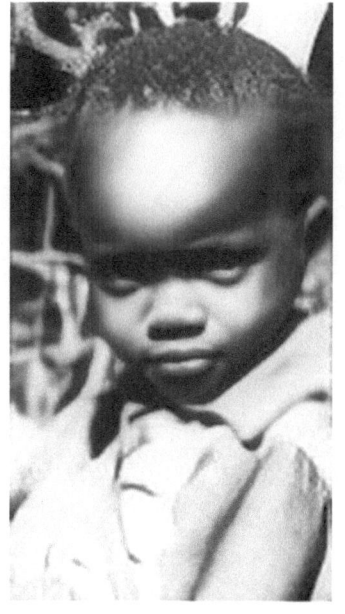

What makes us unique as human beings?

Sometimes I wonder what would have happened if all of us were born in the same part of the world and given similar opportunities. Upbringing, hospitals, schools, universities, basic needs, comfortable homes, loving parents, adequate food, manners, how to behave towards each other... These are some of the basic needs that are taken for granted by many people, yet are vital for any person.

LOOKING BACK TO MOVE FORWARD

Certainly, if you have not travelled outside to a third-world country and seen it all, then it may be a tale and I do not blame you if you do not get it. Those of you who have travelled or have been born elsewhere and migrated to Australia or another part of a civilised country would understand what it is to have a meal, access free healthcare and clean water, feel safe from war and access all other basic needs.

Everyone has a different story that they can tell about themselves and their upbringing. These experiences shape us to be who we are and how we see the world through our lens.

Some people's experiences may be similar, while others are unique. The first time I tasted chocolate was when I moved to Australia. Each time I mention this to my Aussie counterparts, they are completely shocked.

I had seen *Cadburys* chocolate a few times in the shop but never had a chance to taste it because my parents couldn't afford to buy us. Even now, each time I taste a small piece of chocolate, I get covered with numerous pimples on my chin (just like a teenager) that leave dark marks as a reminder that it is not required – so, I don't eat it.

After living in Australia, I found that some children get it a bit easy, although not everyone. For example, going to fancy schools or attending universities where fees are paid for them, but they still blame their parents instead of embracing that opportunity to make the best out of it. Some young adults will even make their parents arrange driving lessons and find a job for them, get their first homes and cars purchased for them, support them when getting married and help raise their kids.

DISPARITIES AND EXPERIENCES

This may contribute largely to a lack of understanding because there is someone there to do it all for you. How do I, as an immigrant, explain to them in easy terms to be grateful, tough and resilient unless this is already in their awareness without them feeling offended?

When these are not fought for, it is easy for them to think that life is easy and let opportunities slide away – only to realise when it is too late what they wasted.

On the other hand, if you worked hard for all these ; using your initiative, for paying your tuition fees, finding accommodation by yourself, and saving any extra coin to clear a car bill, you appreciate the complexity of life and its struggles.

I acknowledge that no one chose where to be born – or the opportunities at their hand – and on the positive, we should all be able to accept, assimilate and learn from each other, appreciating what each one of us brings to the table. I also know that some people went through hell and more dangerous experiences than I did, and so we should all be aware of that.

I had never seen a toothbrush or toothpaste until it was written on my secondary school shopping list. I used to brush my teeth on our way to school using twigs from a tree named *'Commiphora Africana'* – we all did this in my home and embraced it as normal. Birds also love eating the seeds once they grew fruits.

Growing up, we never saw clean water. We used to run miles away to a creek that would be full if it had rained – with reports of several drownings. There were also deep caves with water trapped from the rain where it looked clearer. With no adult in sight, we would reach down to fetch it to fill our *calabashes* and guards with a guarantee that if you slipped in, you would drown with no way of retrieving your body from the deep cave.

From a young age, we were taught to obey, and harsh punishments were administered by both family and teachers at school with a fierce primary school principal – if there was a deviation. My dad didn't know how to nurture. Perhaps they were not taught any other way, so there were just the struggle and the pressure to push us to be better through education. He did not seek an alternative.

Due to such upbringing, one of my brothers completely adopted this way of treating his siblings, wife and his children. He reaches for branches and whacks us all if he feels wronged. He does not know compassion or understanding. He treats people with fists to the ground if you cross his path; it has always been hard to relate with him because no one has been able to look him in the eye to question his behaviour. Mum has been asking him to stop while she walks the other direction to avoid rattling him. Sometimes he heeds her warnings, other times they fall on deaf ears.

In Australia, there are so many jobs and trade opportunities with many colleges offering certificate-level entries where anyone can work their way up to the qualification they want with the right mindset. This is a huge disparity, especially in our village with few options for entry levels to colleges and universities afar. That means you would have to try hard to get admission into a public university to access government support unless you can afford bribes and hefty tuition fees.

When you go overseas, most people back home forget that money does not grow on trees. Their impression is that you are well-off, and you can support them to meet their basic needs. It might be some form of belief engraved in all of us – perhaps even some form of

DISPARITIES AND EXPERIENCES

trauma that we can't shake off. People back home do not understand that we must work tirelessly in this fast-paced environment to earn a living, we have mortgages and have dependents that need ongoing appointments and everyday living demands. Luckily, opportunities are at hand if you like to keep busy to move forward.

I speak for most foreign people that send money to support families, extended families, neighbours and friends we long knew overseas. If we speak to these people on the phone, they tell us with concern how bad their situation has been. Sick family members, a child that needs school fees, pre-wedding or funeral funds and so many other touching conversations that send us on a whirlwind of thoughts to try and send them that money to get the urgent problem fixed. We are used to this and it does not sound strange when they spell it all out – because we are not an individual, we are a community.

When you come from a village back home, you belong to them, a part of a community where they know you from afar. It has never been "those children are for so and so" – instead, it is said that they are "our children" and they expect support.

How many people feel this kind of guilt and pressure or conceivably another type of pressure if they fail those who look up to them?

Perhaps due to taking over parental responsibilities and others' burdens. I learnt to be caring, dependable, and resilient. It helps in some ways to be able to depend on your siblings, family and friends knowing that no matter what, they will stick by you, they have your back and that is what we have always done for each other.

I am aware that most siblings go through ups and downs and that is healthy because, at the end of the day, I do believe that differences in siblings strengthen their relationships. I am also aware that some siblings have chosen to keep it for themselves due to them wanting their space and being left alone. This is also okay because it means that boundaries have been set that have been successful and that is wonderful.

I grew up in a rough environment with a strict father. A retired cop who beat us for anything. He was a protectionist in our interactions with our peers in a harsh way. I lived to fear him and never wanted to be home when he was there because I feared making a mistake and being beaten. I do not know what my other siblings say although I don't think they were treated in any special way. I was not fostered to think independently to make a choice or express myself – until I grew up and had no choice but to trust my instincts. I have been embracing a recovery journey that is a work in progress to reset it all and harmonise.

Later in life, I learnt that if I did not fear Dad, I might have slipped and fallen pregnant or gotten married in my teens. This would have been unfortunate, not only to me but to my family, my village and the community. This might contradict some children's questions about taking their decisions away from them, however, a balance must be found.

Following the harsh guidance coming from a good place, although the administration was not kind, it worked to restrict me until I matured to be able to choose what was good for me. In my defence, I saw many girls drop out in my village due to a lack of guidance and education and persistence. They ended up struggling with life challenges and fell through. They never got a second chance to change their dysfunctional family cycle.

I asked my mum one day what difference it would have made if one of my closest childhood friends got a chance like me. She answered

DISPARITIES AND EXPERIENCES

that perhaps the girl would have done better in life and would have claimed her place with independence. But her chance was lost, and we cannot dwell on the past. Such conversations with Mum have never stopped.

I still talk to my mum about many other missed opportunities for her growing up. She says that although she was not very fortunate, she is proud of raising us and what her children are becoming, she feels accomplished and content.

One of Mum's most encouraging phrases is that, *"Tough times do not last, tough people do."* She is a tough woman and she is right.

Growing up, we did not have a choice of what we chose to do. There was no alternative food to eat and no spare room to run to when the noise became unbearable in our common room. We only had one common room which had a bedroom, kitchen and living room. We had an outside pit latrine with no paper to use. We had to use leaves or sticks to clean – this is still the case for many families at present. We slept in one big handmade shelf bed with no mattress, but a mat made of palm leaves woven by Mum using her calloused hands. It was so rough on our backs, but we had to squeeze in here for safety and comfort.

Women used to make baskets, clothes, and anything by their hand to sell for income or for personal use. We used kerosene lanterns with a wick to add light – with no guarantee of lighting some days, due to the lack of kerosene. We refurbished the house pictured on the book cover from mud and thatch where my siblings and I grew up in.

Women would solely have to cement the floor of their mud houses using cow dung that was pounded in water and mixed with ash from wood charcoal. This would make a thick smooth mixture that would be smeared on the floor and the walls of the house. The mixture would smell for a few days before it dried up, but it meant keeping cracks at bay that harboured scorpions, snakes and other harmful creatures.

Failure to use this dung on the floor would result in having red dirt on everything – including our lungs as the wind would blow over the dirt into the house. We would fetch firewood and would store fire using cow dung and bury it with ash to rekindle the next day because we did not have matches.

I remember many a time walking to the neighbour's home to borrow some fire to prepare food.

I did not have a change of underpants, clothes, shoes or basic things. We did not have soap to wash these. Many children in my village are still affected by this disparity. Their parents do not have a means of feeding, clothing them or lighting their homes.

Water is still fetched by many from a creek that is contaminated by the hospital's upstream where it is used as a sewer system to dump all wastes including needles – only for people to drink it downstream and end up sick with various diseases. There are no testing clinics or laboratories to test for diseases back in our community.

If anyone gets sick, it is assumed that they are sick of either a 'cold' or 'malaria', and therefore, treatment is the same. There is an ongoing unnecessary loss of many young lives.

In my childhood, I did not have any toys or a place to play, a swing unless from tree vines or ropes and slides from fallen trees. We had to be creative – like the soccer ball we made from plastic paper with some strings from tree barks peeled off.

DISPARITIES AND EXPERIENCES

I was a bed wetter until I was about eight years old. I remember the nights used to be challenging. I would wake up with my clothes and rugs all saturated between my siblings (Gideon and Flo), and they did not appreciate the soaking and the smell. Not to mention going to school in the same clothes and staying in them the whole day while peers made fun of me.

In these conditions, we did not escape from nasty creatures like bed bugs. It was common to wake up in the middle of the night with itchy bottoms, we tossed and turned but we couldn't brush them off as they hid back so quickly! The *jiggers* would infest our toes, we had to find those strong acacia thorns to use in picking the jiggers skilfully not to burst their eggs encapsulated in their cocoons because they would infest us back. The same house we slept in stunk as we had harvested crops in one corner in bags where rats and mice would pee around every night; the smell was unbearable. Mice attract snakes, so they often slithered through in our sleep. I am talking of red-belly snakes that are highly venomous. Spotted severally at night and some during the days. Some chickens would just die of their smell even without having been bitten we thought. As a child, I was intrigued and frightened at the same time.

There were cockroaches everywhere, mosquitos carrying malaria that would infect and make us sick for weeks. Dad would force us to chew *chloroquine*, a tablet that is used to treat malaria before we swallowed it, it didn't taste very nice, it was bitter. Head lice were rampant; so much so that we would sit and inspect each other's head, pick and crush them with our fingers.

Mum reminds me of the time when I was very sick as a child. She took me to the nearest health centre. I was given some bags of medicine through the canula. Two weeks later, I recovered but all my baby teeth fell out, the remaining ones turned into brown stumps that I could not use. Luckily, my adult teeth emerged. They had nicknamed me a *"witchetty grub"*. I still get called so by older relatives and Mum's friends.

When I turned eight, I caught measles that was introduced to us after our neighbour's children had it. We were not encouraged to scratch our eyes despite the redness and the itch due to the fear of losing them. My stepmother had to catch a rooster and chop some of its comb off to smear the blood into my eye. The blood was believed to soothe the eye and save it from the catastrophe of the disease. I don't know if it helped or not.

Growing up, dishes were washed in muddy and dirty creek water contaminated upstream. Boreholes ran dry or were too expensive to dig requiring equipment that is still not easily accessible. We had to figure out what to do to make our food as children, no one showed us how. Basic food to sustain us took hours to gather and prepare. By then, we would be starving.

These challenges were not chosen; it was what we had to live with and embrace as a normal part of growing up, without reference to any other child or country having it any different. I had a habit of finding freshly laid warm chicken or bird eggs and I would crack and eat them raw as a day's meal as I didn't know how to cook them at the time. I certainly didn't know about salmonella poisoning! Rotten eggs would crack on my hands with a big pop sound and stink the whole house out for days – trust me you do not want to be near a rotten egg when it pops.

One day in grade six, two of my classmates asked me if they could come home with me for lunch. I was not able to tell them that I slept hungry the previous night or that Mum was not home to make us lunch. I did not consider myself game enough to bear the

DISPARITIES AND EXPERIENCES

shame of saying, *"Hey, hang on, you can't come home because I do not have anything to give you, myself or my siblings for lunch."*

I took them home although there was nothing in our house to eat. I went to my stepmother's house where I got two cups of fermented millet porridge for these girls, and I did not have a cup for myself as there was not enough, I had a couple of mouthfuls from their cups but that was not enough to return to school for the afternoon session.

At the time, I did not see the need to complain because I did not have a choice presented to me to take. For my mum, putting up food on the table was hard enough, let alone complaining about not having anything to eat for days. We never returned a word to our parents or raise our hands to them to fight back when we didn't get our way.

Children were watched from afar, your behaviour was known by the villagers if you were a well-behaved child or if bad mannered, you would be brought into line by the elders. They took responsibility to keep the community safe, they could often use their Swahili proverb saying that, *"Asiyefunzwa na mamake, hufunzwa na ulimwengu"* – meaning that if a child is not taught manners by their mother, they would be taught by the world.

The world is the elders, or the police if their manners were out of hand with no compromise. That is what we were always reminded of to keep us on track.

This expectation played a big role in taming children in a manner that was expected, hence not many criminals were witnessed in the community at the time, although there was ongoing family violence that was never questioned. They also used another Swahili saying.

LOOKING BACK TO MOVE FORWARD

"Mtoto umleavyo, ndivyo akuavyo" – meaning that the way the child is brought up is the way they grow up like.

I believe that although there were hardships in my upbringing, these have shaped me into the grown woman I am. We can sit and look back at experiences that were not so nice and get stuck there but there is no use because that is past. I believe in passing my knowledge and experiences onto my children and anyone who finds a line that is helpful to them, to guide them in the best way possible.

Growing up, we were never encouraged to cry. If you did, you would get a smack. We were not supposed to express any emotional pain or vulnerability and we were told to toughen up. For my boys, I will teach them about the expectations as humans and ensure they keep on track. I do know that it is their call to choose the right path with good guidance, but they would certainly find it hard to grow up in my village.

I hope that they will continue to learn about their lineage and if they wish to go back to experience their origin, they would be supported. No one has a manual for raising children – I tend to think that I am doing enough by raising emotionally balanced children, putting food on the table and taking them to school. I am doing the right thing, by being their parent. It is their responsibility to take on the world with the resources available and stay away from the company that will lead them astray.

We couldn't demand anything from our parents and birthdays were never known or celebrated, but there were other cultural celebrations like circumcision ceremonies that played an important part of a child's upbringing. Those who have travelled to Kenya, Africa or overseas know for sure how appreciative these people are when they see a foreigner.

DISPARITIES AND EXPERIENCES

They are creatures of curiosity. They like to be friendly and make people feel welcome and to feel at home. They love to know how far it is from where you live, the time difference and about your family. They will welcome you with a big smile whether they did not eat last night or slept on the ground. They share anything they have left and do not say that the food is not enough to give to the visitor, they give it with all their heart and have the most beautiful and welcoming energy. They will entertain you and hope you travel back home safely and remember the good experience and the people you met when you go back to your country.

That is the African spirit.

Chapter Two

MY PHILOSOPHY IN LIFE

I believe that there is no permanent situation. I also believe in treating others the way you'd like to be treated. That is how I view life.

I believe that there is always an option to a situation or another path to getting there. I found that life may throw issues and experiences that might come to flatten you, but that is not the end of it. The trick is exploring what works for you with the courage to take the chance, reminding yourself that no matter how hard the situation gets, you are going to make it.

It is easy to fear and to slump your shoulders and leave yourself in darkness, looking to take the easy path. If you choose that, life will not lend you a helping hand. You will start going silent when your

LOOKING BACK TO MOVE FORWARD

friend's message to check on you. It may go on for months or even years. It may feel like you will never get in control of this dark cloud or feel normal again. Consequently, you might end up feeling halted from your strong go-getter attitude to being reduced to nothing.

The truth is that there are ways around these situations. Although it is tough to see the alternative during the crisis due to the stress, we must do the work ourselves to get back on our feet again. We all know that life is not a rehearsal, and it is unlikely that you will get lucky without trying. All the hard work you put in will steer you into the *luck* and the *blessings* you are seeking.

Whatever the challenge that comes your way, I am here to remind you that there will always be a solution, a reprieve. If a negative experience crosses your path, it is a way to test your strength and agility. To see how fast you can figure it out and pass through it. Some experiences do not require us to do much, it can just be a matter of getting out of that house and taking a short walk that we already know of but lack the drive to do it.

MY PHILOSOPHY IN LIFE

Maybe we have been working so hard and our bodies just require staying in the house and doing nothing. In stillness and coldness, to let your heart, body and mind catch up with each other to create harmony to find that amnesty. It may be those frozen moments we get to know ourselves better in a deeper understanding to foster self-love and compassion for our injured souls to find the strength to carry on.

Other times may be calling a trusted colleague, or the person you need to speak to, to clear a misunderstanding to have a peaceful night than toss and turn over it. Maybe it is not overexplaining yourself because nothing needs to be said or done to prove your worth or your innocence. Perhaps saying no is all you need as your saving grace – say it.

Whether it is going out and staring up at the sky, searching for that moving cloud or jumping in your car and finding a footpath far from your home that you can walk along. Maybe it is standing up for yourself, your colleagues, your partner, your children, or anyone you see struggling by being mistreated or not being heard, so you know that you have contributed positively to changing their lives and that is very good of you.

Be proud of yourself because that is some form of unique accomplishment in making the world a better place. My thoughts are that change ought to be manifested in challenging times.

When I look back, I have passed through a lot. Nothing was handed over to me on a silver platter since my childhood, I always had to work hard for it, and I still do not know an option.

I know many people would resonate with this, depending on their various paths in life.

LOOKING BACK TO MOVE FORWARD

The only option I know is the courage to have a go at it. I would put it out that to manoeuvre life situations, one requires courage and guts. Sometimes the path may never come to an end, and you may never get a closure depending on the situation – but you may get a short break, a reprieve, and that is okay. Hang on to that which makes you feel better.

Along my path, I found out that we do not become strong by masking discomfort. Furthermore, we do not move on by masking the hardships we faced pretending that everything is okay and that we are not heartbroken. Rather, we acknowledge and own these tough experiences and use them as fuel to overcome the hill that you must climb to see past. I use my past experiences to get me past any hurdle, not prepared to be thrown out because, to me, the worst has already passed.

If you keep calm when responding to difficult situations, it does not mean that you have not faced or experienced hardship. It is the creativity that comes with the experiences, and you must be willing to be vulnerable with an understanding that there will be something great and magical that is variegated between these broken pieces of yourself. It also means that you have acknowledged that your needs matter and need to be met at some level by you.

I have seen a few very strong friends, my clients and colleagues opening up deeply and feeling comfortable crying in front of me, alone having a cup of tea. I acknowledge their hurt and their worry. In my heart, I know I must step up and listen and be the shoulder to cry on and help in any way I can because they trust me. They can sit and cry in front of me because they know I have solace; I do not judge, and I embrace vulnerability because I know the path I have walked.

MY PHILOSOPHY IN LIFE

What you make out of your tough upbringing or experiences can be life-changing.

In most of my experiences, picturing myself as a gazelle helps me remember to have some self-compassion. I remind myself that, *"Gosh, today I do not feel like a lioness."*

I take the gazelle path and it works for me because gazelles run fast because they know they have a purpose. In the jungle, even the hungriest lion cannot keep pace with a strong gazelle. Just like me, I run straight, I take people literally, and I trust easily. If you hurt me intentionally, I take the lioness path and do the necessary steps to let you know why it was not okay and why I have kept my distance.

Some situations that I have encountered have been more than challenging, but the results always showed me how courageous I was to be able to tolerate the uncertainty. Those are the paths I have taken, mostly solely and it seems when I think and take the necessary steps, I can do it without depending on others to make a choice then it is almost certainly safe for me because it involved compassion for myself.

Let's say you've been promised something during a conversation by someone you considered to have formed a good relationship with. For example, *"Oh, if you need work, I would be more than happy to look into that, just send me your resume,"* or, *"Yeah if you need a chat, just message me and we will talk."*

What happens after you do as you were asked to? Does the promise always get fulfilled each time when you take the offer? What about if it doesn't? How does it feel to be let down? It is important to think through each promise we offer to ensure that we stand by it.

LOOKING BACK TO MOVE FORWARD

I came to realise that we all thrive with reassurance and safety from childhood. Whether as children or adults, if this line is broken, then we hurt inside. I take such information very seriously. Partly because I am not living with my family, I trust easily those I encounter on my journey. I am aware that we can still give and get nothing in return, and that sometimes the choices we stick by may be the easier ones – although we know they will lead us nowhere or astray.

My hope is that you will use the line that resonates with you, to help you go past the hurdle. Maybe you have found a different line – use it because we are all in this world to discover what works best for us.

Chapter Three

GROWING UP

Just like everyone else in the village, we were children brought up in red-dirt, mud houses who seemed lost most of the time.

Although tough, it was beautiful. The dirt smelled nice outside, especially when it rained. We could smell the rain from afar. There used to be beautiful creatures that came out of the dirt that we played with; I cannot pick which one was better than the other because they were all unique. The wildflowers blossomed with different smells filling the air.

I come from a polygamous family where my dad married three wives who lived in the same compound, raising 19 children among them. My mum was the third wife and by the time we came along, we were almost the youngest – except for our elder brothers.

LOOKING BACK TO MOVE FORWARD

Polygamy is a tradition that is still acceptable in most countries in Africa where men are allowed to marry as many wives as they wish.

The three wives had their own houses and Dad had his own separate house but in the same compound. They used to go and see him when they were supposed to. My stepmothers got along with us all; they had similar birth names (Njau) and they cared for all of us.

Although each of the wives used to look after their own children as best as they could, they had some spare time for all the other stepchildren. Between caring for their well-grown children, they could occasionally check on us and share their food with us when Mum had to travel to the farm, leaving us alone for weeks or months before she returned with food on her back.

I don't know what was going in their minds after the second and the third wife was married. I did not hear them make a fuss unless it happened among themselves without exposing it to the children. Perhaps they liked that they shared responsibilities and consoled each other during tough times. I never heard them question Dad about endless children coming along later – perhaps they had embraced this as normal from what they had seen.

This continues to impact many women in different communities in Kenya and Africa, but little is said and done.

However, as beautiful as Kenya is, there is a multitude of issues that are still engrained in some of the men's worlds that continue to empower them to reach their misogynist peaks. The men in political positions and power are also culprits, unfortunately, not many have a sense of intuition inside of them.

Nothing is there for women to empower themselves unless they take their own initiative.

My insight here is for anyone in Australia to recognise how lucky they are to have freedom of choice and expression because their rights are protected.

Sadly, the village girl does not have a voice unless she is empowered through education to look far beyond a Kenyan or an African man's perspective.

Growing up, we had to take turns in herding the animals. Herding meant leading a big flock of animals consisting of goats, sheep and cows far away from home and ensuring that we ran all day round to keep them in check around the paddocks. The animals used to be spread out in the field that was filled with acacia trees and other shrubs which had thorns and prickles. We just had to hop past these barefoot.

If we took our eyes off them, they would take off or cross the road to the adjacent paddocks.

There were mainly no fences and most neighbours had crops growing meaning if one of the animals crossed and ate their crop, it would cause trouble for my dad. It would also mean that the neighbour's crop was consumed and that was a big loss.

The neighbour would have to come to my dad to report it and – well, you guessed it – the beating would follow with possibly no food and other threats of being told to go grazing again the next day instead of going to school.

Later in the afternoon, we were required to lead the animals to the river that was in another region some miles away. During hot months, we used to love leading them to the river where we would swim. We would jump in by a cliff and dive deep, not only to cool down, but we would also be quenching our thirst straight from the river. The river was full all year round back then – Mum says that it almost dries up now until the rains are back due to people pumping water to their homes upstream.

Walking around the house during the night, was scary because there was no lighting to see ahead. The compound was full of all sorts of harsh creatures like spiders, scorpions and occasional brown snakes; none of their bites was pleasant. Scorpion bites are terrible.

If you get stung by one, it can go either way. Either you react to them, or you are fine. I remember how miserable it felt when I got stung. It felt to me like one had gotten inside my finger and it was running amok round and round. It was so painful it took the entire night to settle with no pain medication to help.

GROWING UP

There were highly venomous brown snakes and puff adders. We were lucky to have survived without snake bites because these were not survivable. Most brown snakes would slither and go past when we slept, but luckily did not attack. We were mindful not to step or roll on one. You would occasionally spot puff adders with a rattle tail under a tree waiting for a bird to step on a branch – you could see them curled up and shooting up to catch a bird like an arrow.

We had to learn to milk the animals. With a jug in one hand and our fingers to the action. We would have to ensure both fingers gripped and extracted milk correctly, ensuring we aimed inside the jug with no waste.

At times, we would milk directly into our mouths to satisfy our hunger with warm milk from the cows' teats. If we ever argued about any chores instructed by Dad, we would get beaten and would have to find a place to sleep with no food.

In my culture, there are strict norms that children are supposed to follow. If you don't follow them, you would be spanked. For example, crying for anything or feeling entitled. If you refused food offered to you, if you ate at your neighbours' house, returned home after sunset, slept in while the elders have woken up, sat on a chair when an elder was standing, stared at an elder when they talked to you instead of staring on the ground. If the teacher reported you to your parents, listening to conversations between elders or using inappropriate language.

You would be beaten up if you stumbled and fell on the ground if you broke an egg, dropped food or anything else by accident. Talking back to an elder, having an elder repeat what they already said or if Dad called you for the second time. The list is endless.

Amid all these traditions, Mum has never laid her hand on any of us even when we did not follow the rules. I think it helped that she gave us a well of love to counteract the fear we harboured daily.

My stepsiblings got along to some extent when we were growing up, although some have branched out and kept a distance because as times change, so do people. My elder brother says he grew up and was sharing a bed with our elder stepbrothers during their time and has kept a close bond to date.

In some way, you can say my family was huge and spread, well-known from the boundaries of our community. We were taught to be respectful to our stepmothers and their children and never fought with our stepsiblings. We lived in peace with hardly any conflicts – except in later years when the time came for land subdivision after Dad passed.

Land inheritance conflicts are very common, especially for families who rely on them. Those who can leave family land and purchase land elsewhere have inner peace.

Growing up, children underwent a series of rites of passage to transition them from childhood to youth and then to adult life. There was no baptism or christening but the children had to study the Bible to be baptised and confirmed. They would have to undergo a series of Bible studies and be tested to qualify for confirmation to keep their baptism name. The reason for the Bible study was for the children to learn about the Bible and understand the teachings to be accountable for their actions and sins before they can start receiving the holy communion.

I grew up in a Methodist church, and this helped shape my values in a way. The Bible study test questions were tough, but everyone

GROWING UP

had to pass before confirmation to keep our baptismal names – which are mostly English due to colonisation by the British. I got my name Lillian confirmed after being called Anna for a few months in my lower primary school days.

Our village was occupied mainly by people who spoke my mother tongue, Kitharaka, and rarely did we have people outside the community living in our village. This is now changing with the nearest shopping centre, Marimanti, thriving with additional shops as a cosmopolitan place with people travelling from afar to take government jobs.

There were some societal norms and traditions which were practised in the village for both girls and boys, and I certainly know that my two boys would struggle to fit in with some of the rites.

This is what my brothers were subjected to, an initiation process' a transition from childhood to boyhood in a ceremony called *'Kumerua'*.

Around age 10, the boy is taken away at the darkest of the night by men to the riverbanks to be swallowed by a monster called *'Kirirmo'* – while women were strictly kept at bay. When signalled by men at the riverbank, Kirimo would be invited to swallow the boy whole and keep the boy in his belly for a few hours and it was by sheer chance if a boy could make it out alive.

Women were not informed exactly what was happening to the boy – not even the mother knew. This night, we could hear colossal noise that sounded like an amplified sound made from a didgeridoo. It was so loud it could echo from miles away. But the echo for me reminded me that my brother was still alive and hopefully safe.

The monster from the African jungle who came to the riverbanks at night was a one-legged big giant with one eye. It was supposed to swallow this boy that night for a few hours so that the boy could learn lessons to be tough in life.

Women were told that there were millions of ants and scorpions in the monster's stomach which would bite all over the boy's body hard enough that when he gets retched back, he would be covered in welts from the bites. When the boy returned home in the early hours of the morning, he had welts all over his body, bruises and marks. The boy was required to stay inside the house until the welts resolved, and these would clear up by the third day.

I am sure we can all guess where the welts were from… Men take an oath not to disclose this act, and they take this secret to their graves.

Later, when the boys turned 15, they would be required to undergo circumcision. A ceremony that is expected to be a normal rite of passage to qualify to be an adult. The circumcision process is done in a traditional ceremony with no anaesthetics or antibiotics with the expectation to transition the boy to a man.

These practices are embedded in our tradition and culture and have a dire psychological effect on any young boy. Not least the trauma from the swallowing experiences or circumcision, but the boys who missed these rites are subject to ridicule from most society members, ultimately leading to unstable emotions to focus well on their psychological and social development.

Amid the crisis of growing up, I have countless fond memories of my childhood that I still treasure. We did not have electricity to light our house so after sunset, we would go straight to bed because it was hard to see in the dark. On other nights, we would sit by the fire with my stepmothers whether Mum was around or not. They would passionately narrate stories whilst they weaved their baskets by the bonfire.

Some of the stories are embedded in me and I tell them to my children. They would teach us how to read the stars, interpret the sky for drought or abundance, and identify the milky way, the plough and many other star formations. We were informed of ancient stories of war and hardships, our origin, our clans and relatives who lived far away from us.

It was beautiful sitting outside at dusk around the bonfires watching the blue skies counting all the twinkling stars and observing many other formations. In my opinion, this played a big role in our upbringing and the person I am today.

The stories instilled humility, endurance and the urge to keep going because there *will* be a better day ahead. These stories taught us resilience that I have continued to hold close to my heart which has gotten me past many life hurdles, including work-related issues that almost crippled my mental state.

Growing up, we had no computers or phones to play with, and I look at children of this age with entitlement and how they react if their iPad is flat or have poor internet connection. They do not know what lacking means; they have no clue. In my childhood, I spent my time worried about where I would find firewood to light a fire to cook my meals that were not easy to prepare. There is such a disparity that is so hard to ignore.

All the play was outdoors with no indoor sport even heard of – I'd never heard of sunscreen until I migrated. We felt safe in our community though. We would spend some weekends swimming across the creek and collecting wild fruits on the banks of the river. Sometimes we had to climb up huge ancient trees to pick fruits up the top. It made the effort worthwhile. Numerous varieties of berries lasted all year round depending on the seasons. Some still exist.

Children's care was mostly a shared responsibility by the community and each child was known by their name from afar. We never got lost but if we wandered away and were found, we would be escorted back home to our parents safely. If a stranger was found to have committed an act of violence of any form towards children, they would be beaten up by a crowd to near-death experience to learn their manners.

Traditionally, men played the drums at night to celebrate harvest or abundance, although I have never seen my dad play any. Mum wove baskets and mats to be used at home to sleep on and sold others in the local markets.

We would braid our hair into cornrows and other designs among ourselves – while Mum used to ensure they were neatly done when she could. We pierced our ears with acacia thorns after scrapping and smoothening to remove the outside coat using sharp knives. The thorn would be left in the piercing and rotated for a few days until the piercing hole healed. Puss used to develop after the second day and would heal with some itch towards the end of the wound healing process. I pierced my own ears.

Men would carve shoes out of old car rubber tyres to wear to keep the scorching heat off their bare feet and thorns. These were considerably cheap and lasted long. It was a big invention where men still use the same pair year-round with no alternative.

Growing up with my siblings and half-siblings, we had our good playful days, and sometimes, we fought for food or something else.

GROWING UP

One day we would fight and be great friends the next. Just like I see most siblings do.

My youngest sister, Maureen, was the slowest eater of all time. My brothers and I would eat all our food fast and then encroach on hers unless an adult stopped us, which mostly was rare as Mum worked away most of the days. Maureen has every right to demand answers and revenge from her siblings for these savage treatments!

A few years ago, I funded Maureen to join me in Australia where she undertook her Nursing Degree and later completed a Master of Nursing. She currently lives and works in Gold Coast, a fast-paced environment and she loves it. To date, she has not discovered how much food there is in Australia; she is still the same and still doesn't eat much. Her eating still sits on par with her decisions, and she takes things easy. She does not rush and mostly makes wise decisions.

It was expected of me to watch over my younger siblings, Gideon, Evans and Maureen, when my elder sister Florence went to deal with other chores and Mum was away.

One morning after Mum left for the markets to buy some items and groceries, Evans started a fight with me. He was used to picking up fights with his older siblings as he liked to tackle people. I was supposed to be watching over them but here I am fighting Evans, while Gideon wandered onto the farm and Maureen sat nearby!

Evans was never afraid and not going to stop when I asked him to. Then boom, he started tackling me as per his talent, and I fell with a reasonable thud onto the ground. We were in a maize cobs farm, so I cleared a few rolling up and down the hill. It was impossible to end this fight – just as well I didn't fracture any bone, but it was lethal for me because I was tall and skinny.

LOOKING BACK TO MOVE FORWARD

He proceeded to sit on me punching me over. Honestly, some children's brains are mostly messed up. We couldn't reason unless an adult was there to get us off each other. When he sat on me and I couldn't roll him over, I got scared. In my brain, I felt like this was it, that I was going to die, and I had to fight this kid back and rescue myself, but I couldn't skilfully push him over as he was too sturdy and was stuck on me.

At some point, I lost it. I picked up a rock that was nearby and hit him on the forehead so hard. The sight of blood gashing through out of his forehead got me even more scared as I thought he would not survive.

What would I say to Mum?

I do not think he felt the pain because he never used to cry when he injured himself, but he started crying when he saw blood dripping out and ran off. That is when I finally got a chance to get up. Now that was not my negotiation skill, but I felt so sad as I was the elder sister looking after him! But no amount of negotiation ever worked.

I was lucky the rock didn't land on his eye, but I must have unlocked a missing piece of the puzzle in his brain because Evans is very smart. He has always been number one in his class throughout primary school and topped his high school marks.

Evans went to university and completed his master's and his PhD, he has acquired numerous fellowships and is currently in the process of migrating. He's a top guy in maths and science – nothing gives him any challenges. He can work out things in his sleep and he is unstoppable. He has grown to be a good fellow who is very dependable and now he is married and a father to two beautiful and smart daughters, Chloe and Ava, who share the same birthday two years apart, which is sensational.

We grew up on the bottom of Dad's hill where most rocks just rolled down and we could go climbing them without shoes. There were huge old trees and big rocks and natural gravity from top to bottom hill. We used to climb up the top of the hill to look for wildlife and eggs from local birds.

Up the top of the hill, you can see the river below meandering downstream. You can see the sunrise and sunset. It is a beautiful and peaceful view that I yearn for even after migrating. Every time I go back home, I hike up to my familiar sensational views. The leaves at the hill change colours every season and this is something I meditate on each time I want to fall asleep quickly or distract myself from a busy lifestyle, I simply take myself back to this hill and visualise the beautiful different colours of the leaves especially the colour changes around December is sensational. This is when most native trees change their leaves colour from green to yellow then orange to red before they dry up and fall off.

I have encountered scorpions and deadly spiders and poisonous snakes on this hill but all lucky to be spared. Between rock climbing and skipping, I fell off a few times and still have numerous childhood scars that remind me of my fun times as a child rolling down the hills. We had fun games and learnt skills like whistling, blowing out of our hands to call for the animals, winking, and shaking our noses and ears like cows, of which I am still an expert at.

As a child and teenager, I did not get options for food choices except for what we farmed. Sometimes, we learnt to live with food and other times, to survive until the next day to have a feed.

LOOKING BACK TO MOVE FORWARD

No option for fussiness and scoring a meal three times a day was almost unheard of.

Most families had to work from one season to another to ensure they produced some staple food for their use which was mainly grains and cereals. A harvest depended on the amount of rain we got that season without irrigation.

For those who were able to afford luxury food, like bread and soda, it was considered exotic. We herded animals but were not able to live off them. Animal meat and stews like goat, sheep, cow or chicken were cooked deliciously with amazing traditional recipes. Essentials like salt and sugar were mainly unavailable in our house and borrowing from neighbours was commonplace, nearing an everyday occurrence.

There are more diverse foods that are cooked with local special spices that are mouth-watering. If you happen to move from one region to another, you will find the local's favourite delicacies.

We had to make flour with our hands using two rocks to grind the grains. It was a tedious job and palms would be filled with blisters and calluses. It would be near impossible to grind for a long time to prepare enough flour to feed all of us.

We had to take turns with Florence to grind. This was by far a terrible chore for me because it was very strenuous, and we hated it. The flour would be used to make fermented porridge or eaten as fresh, and sometimes we could add cows' fermented milk which would make it even more delicious and nutritious. There were local wild vegetables that grew after the rains, which we picked and cooked to mix with the flour to make a thick paste. These kept us going, and we were never lacking in energy or laughter.

GROWING UP

In recent years, most families in my village have adopted a way of milling maize and other locally farmed grains to make flour to prepare meals. Food made from flour is easier to prepare as opposed to boiling maize for many hours to make it edible.

We would walk into a local market with a bag of corn or millet or sorghum and pay some shillings to have this transformed into flour. The grain would be poured into the milling basket and after some loud noise it would come to the other side as flour, I thought it was the best invention that saved the lives of many children, especially those whose teeth aren't yet developed when their mother's milk dried.

As a child, sometimes mum had to chew the hard food using her teeth to soften it for us and stick it back into our mouths. Now, you may question why she would do that.

Do you know why?

She was desperate to feed us. She had young kids holding onto her clothes and legs waiting to be fed and she had nothing to give, with no baby food heard of. When mum's breast milk dried, she had to do what she had to do to feed us.

As a mother, no one would like to watch their children starve to death, and I think Mum was very clever and brave to invent such a method. I don't know who taught her because there were no midwives involved during our time. I saw something else she did, too. If a child had a cold with a blocked nose desperate for air, she would use her mouth to suction that and spit out – making her a champion! We had no cough syrup to use or *Vicks* to rub to unblock our congested chests and noses.

LOOKING BACK TO MOVE FORWARD

In recent years, there have been a lot of tourists who go to Kenya and have brought with them some international ideas and recipes making it diverse in most dishes served in cafes and restaurants...

The signature is to ask for the original *'Nyama Choma'* (charcoal grilled meat) with *'Kachumbari'* (salsa) and *'Ugali'* (maize flour pound). It has always been a favourite and I must eat it each time I visit home.

For those children who are so fussy like my son Oliver going through phases of childhood hurdles, just remember it was not easy for me, my siblings and most of the other children. It is not easy out there. Some children got it even tougher and worse off than us.

For anyone criticising this upbringing, perhaps yours was easier and more regulated with adequate food as a bare basic. We still count our blessings to be alive and have survived, having a mother who tried her best and gave us the absolute best of her ability. She got no appreciation and no validation for all that she did for us. She gave us nothing but love despite all the hardships she went through – resulting in her heavy alcohol and tobacco use to escape and keep her head above the water.

I watched many children around us starve due to famine after their mothers gave up.

Chapter Four

MUM

Janet. She is a smart, resilient and beautiful woman; the third and youngest wife to my Dad. Mum is my maternal warrior. She gave birth to eight children, four boys and four girls, she lost one daughter when little but seven of us lived, thrived and we all have our stories to share. We all grew up in one house she had built, until the boys were of age to move out while girls remained in the original house, refurbished it and shared it with Mum until we were old enough to go our separate ways.

We grew to call her *'Mugeni'* throughout our lives, instead of Mum. Mugeni means a guest or a new visitor in our mother tongue, and to my culture, it meant a new addition to Dad's wives. Our stepsiblings would have started to call her by this name and when we came along, we just continued. She didn't mind us calling her Mugeni.

LOOKING BACK TO MOVE FORWARD

We all grew up tending and helping each other to be our best, despite the hardships. Mum was our rock; she never gave up. Sometimes I wonder what it would have been like if she got an opportunity to attend school. I have asked her many a time what difference it would have made if she got an opportunity to study. I tend to think that she would have made a fantastic life for herself and her children, and she agrees. But she did not get this choice to attend school because she was a woman who was not allowed to go to school.

Mum grew up amongst her three brothers. As a girl and young woman, she felt that she was all alone in her family. She was a woman and was not recognised as important as her brothers. Whilst her brothers were supported to attend school, she was forced to tend to them and herd the animals daily. She would ensure when the boys came home they had food. Her brothers had a choice for support, and one became a teacher. Mum couldn't make a life for herself other than getting married as a young teen to my dad who would have been more than twice her age – Mum was younger than some of dad's older children.

Her mother (my grandmother) passed on while Mum was married to my dad. I remember my grandmother's face vaguely; she was not in great health, but she loved us. Mum knew that she was marrying an older man who had two wives already. I would think that she needed to feel safe out of her home, to look for opportunities to be better in life. She was used to serving, and this was not an exception.

Mum had a busy life raising three girls and four boys, I was in the middle, the fourth born, she protected us as much as she could, although it was a rollercoaster and a chaotic life of poverty and deprivation. It was a struggle for Mum to make a life for us and herself, being a teenager herself when she got married, she was still learning how to care for a man way older than her and look after her children at the same time. She did not know how to say no or question if something was not good for her; she learnt to accept and keep going.

Mum was obedient, she thought she married her hero, perhaps due to the hardships she had faced in her own home. Mum was not nurtured – no wonder she found an old policeman whom she thought would rescue her. This was a common practice for many other women to be married as a second wife, or third, even fourth, depending on what the men wanted. It was all about men, and it still is today mostly, with minimal change.

Traditional roles for women were to serve their men, be home to look after the children and animals, be submissive and be the care providers. That is what I saw. There were and still are not many shared roles back home and no options for careers available then especially if you were born in the village. Women would be the ones tilling the farms using primitive handheld tools to clear, cultivate and plant crops, weed and harvest to feed their husbands and children.

Mum did all these chores, on top of keeping her children safe. She was our provider, and a confidant importantly; she made sure that we all felt loved. My mum hid most of her struggles from us, she never yelled or lashed out.

Mum was away from us most of our growing life, she used to walk for over 30 or more kilometres to the farm where she would stay for a few weeks, even months, tilling, planting and cultivating and harvesting. She did not know any other way to provide for us, rather than work tirelessly and walk home when she could. She had built an old mud and thatch shack where she would stay on the farm while away, alone in the forest, in the middle of nowhere. Perhaps, she found a break and refuge of quietness away from chaos at home.

We visited the farm during school holidays and weekends to help Mum cultivate. We would all have hand tools and measure 10 by 10 steps square to weed before we could get a break. There was no need to complain after seeing how much land needed to be weeded, so we just got on with the task in the scorching sun.

It was the nights that were frightening. We slept in this shack that could not shut or lock at night. It was the same room we stored the harvest before transporting it home. There were mice and snakes at times, dangerous for all of us. But we had no other place to stay. It had to be aired constantly to ensure air circulation. It was not so good when it rained because if it was windy, we would all get saturated, and the roof would leak as it had been made from grass thatch.

MUM

When we travelled back home on a long journey, we would all carry a bag each on our backs with either maize or any other type of food Mum had harvested in the season. We would walk the whole day and arrive at dark. I still don't understand why there were no easier options of acquiring food.

During the rainy season, it was dangerous crossing flooded rivers infested with crocodiles on our feet whilst carrying luggage. If we slipped off, there was no way to survive the raging river and a waterfall just meters away downstream. We got used to this and never complained about it because there was no other way of accessing meals at the time; we had to work for it.

When Mum was away, we lived each day at a time with no expectations other than surviving. We had to look after ourselves and lived to find food for our stomachs as children with no parent to feed us for months. I can count a few times when Dad made us food. He was there to punish us if things didn't go per his expectations. For example, if we didn't cook or boil maize for ourselves and him, if we refused to herd or if we did something wrong at school.

Florence, my elder sister, is the third born. She was and still is a strong woman, a good, reliable, caring and hardworking sister who would occasionally look after us when Mum was not at home. Some days when there was food to prepare, she would wake up early, cook and feed her three young siblings, and prepare us and herself to go to school. This role continued from primary and secondary school. I would imagine she was not that mature to know what to do with most of her chores. She just had to do what she could to sustain us; this is what we all knew. Hunter-gatherer as children, building resilience.

If you come to think of it here in Australia, it would be child protection and a safety issue for most families.

LOOKING BACK TO MOVE FORWARD

Over time from the hardships, Mum turned into an alcoholic to try and escape from this reality. I would only imagine what was going through her mind. Maybe even having dark thoughts that she never disclosed to us. She found the comfort of where to turn to when things didn't turn out as she hoped; alcohol. She would drink herself to sleep on cheap local brews made from fermented grains or some other type of fermented sugar cane juice.

I also know how to make these because I still have the recipes in my head from helping Mum prepare them. I have drunk these when hungry several times, mostly up to the third day of the fermentation process, when they are semi-sweet and sour – but don't mention it to Mum!

After the brew hits the third day of fermentation, you must leave it to the experts because it starts to become strongly sour. By the seventh day, it is at this stage it has the drunkenness effects when these people like it because it makes them very drunk – quickly. The process is sophisticated because they use grains through to a seventh-day process of adding ingredients as required until it matured. There were no chemicals involved, just pure grain flour and mixtures.

I do not know how much Mum consumed to put her off stress for the night, but the next morning, she would be up at about 3am, and leave at dusk to walk to the farm which was located miles from home. She did not have an alarm; I would imagine it was the rebound effect!

Drinking in the village by both men and women was and still is a common way to escape their stressful reality or a way to socialise with village mates. Dad was no exception, he used to drink too much and mostly turned physical – although I did not quite understand his reasons for drinking because I didn't think he had any visible responsibilities. Unless he hid the stress in the quiet because most responsibilities were reputed by the three wives he had.

I remember Mum getting so stressed some days because she couldn't feed us, she would say, *"I have nothing, there is no food, and I have to return to the farm."*

She was heartbroken most of the time although she tried hard to keep it together. I have never seen her tears – even when life pushed her so much. Even when Dad beat her up, she would have her shoulders high and her head up. What a strong woman.

I have never seen her get a cuddle from my Dad or anyone. Partly because it was culturally inappropriate to touch or be seen hugging in public. She never expressed her sorrow and didn't enunciate how stressed or worried she was to us. She kept the race up and tried to speak in a firm and reassuring voice so that we wouldn't worry. She would often leave to find us food by working on people's farms for days or months and return with small monies which she would use to purchase basic items of need.

One day, Mum left for the farm and the next night, I saw our elder stepsiblings whispering to each other. We wondered what was happening because they did not want to break any bad news to us.

While in the dark, all in a big confusion, I overheard someone saying in our mother tongue, *"She drank herself to death."*

I could tell it was Mum.

I ran to my sister Florence and said to her that I think Mum drank herself to death at the farm. That night, reports had reached my dad that my mum had passed away on a footpath to her farm. She had been laying down since the previous night and was found in the afternoon, in the scorching sun. When the nearby people saw her on the path, apparently, she was not breathing.

One person who knew her walked miles to relay the message home to Dad because there were no phones to use. No one cared to move her to a shade because they were too scared to touch a dead person. She had been drinking the local brew the previous night at the home adjoining our farm, a few meters from where she was sleeping.

I don't know what brought Mum back to life but when Dad left the following morning with some extended family members, they found her up and already tilling the land, having miraculously recovered and survived whatever the ordeal was.

Whether she was poisoned or in an alcohol-induced coma, it has never been told. She has never spoken at length about the story. Every time I asked her, she dismissed the question and does not like to explain what had happened that day. On a positive, she quit alcohol and tobacco after this incident.

Although her path was not easy, Mum supported and guided us all to our paths. In the end, she had a sense of achievement and pride for raising us. I still use Mum's guidance she gave me when growing up.

Although she struggled to make ends meet for us, she always had time to give us counsel. She instilled the spirit of resilience, kindness and hard work despite the hardships. Mum raised us with compassion regardless of her ongoing struggles, and her trauma.

At the end of our rough patch, we all went through high schools and universities. Three of my brothers have a PhD and the rest of us have master's degrees, which makes me insist that anyone can do it and that all your dreams are valid. Referencing our hardships, if we all did it in our family, if you do not give up, you can all make it irrespective of the obstacles.

A few years ago, after we all finished high school, Mum self-referred to adult education where she successfully studied her basic education, Math, and Swahili which she now speaks fluently on top of our mother tongue. Her teacher always spoke passionately about how motivated Mum was; her self-drive and a fast learner.

I say this is a remarkable effort and achievement for Mum and us all given we were sleeping hungry most nights with no plans of when we would get the next meal. If there was, we cooked and ate the same food for many days and nights without storing this in a fridge. Amazing how salmonella never existed then – or possibly we had adapted to constipation and other stomach bugs.

I call and speak to Mum every few days. We speak about anything, and she guides me if in doubt. Although sometimes she may not make sense of where I am in life and how I feel most of the time because I do not like to burden her with any trouble. I know Mum is always there and she continues to say, *"I am proud of you, I have given you all my blessings, you have a kind heart, and you will be okay."* She thinks I am wise, which is reassuring!

All I can say is that she is right. Mum knows how much kindness, courage and resilience I have had to embrace to be where I am now, and so have all her other children. I am grateful that she has been alive to see us all grow strong, and I am forever honoured to spare my thoughts and a few dollars to send her to buy anything she wants. It has always been my pleasure to share this life with my Mum, looking back at years and years of pure turmoil. She has been hesitant to visit Australia but it's on the cards; soon she will come.

There are a few women that I have read about, some women of colour and others I do not know of, or heard about their experiences in transforming the world. These women have impacted my life in a big way, and I applaud them.

They continue to encourage women from all walks of life, women of colour and others who have experienced hardships in life to not give up. I dig deep into such courageous narratives to get me through any hardship.

Chapter Five

He was a former policeman, 6ft 4. He had numerous siblings born into his polygamous family and he later represented his family in polygamy. All of Dad's siblings might have been polygamous; at least the few that I know. With many pieces of land and a small wage, Dad felt he could marry three wives due to having 'wealth'.

Dad built a home on the slope of a hill from one of his many pieces of land to accommodate his three wives and 19 children, of whom we knew. He had his own house whilst each of his wives had a house of their own. Dad was the area sub-chief; he commanded the village. He was respected as wise and kind and most people from the village came to him for counsel distressed and would go back home satisfied with a solution.

Living with my dad was tough. It was impossible for me to be a child, and I had to mature quickly.

One Sunday evening, I got home a little late from church; it was dark, and I had nowhere to go, so I hid in the house, and Dad waited for me by the entrance. I ran past and hid inside our house behind the door, knowing full well that he would find me.

To say I felt helpless is an understatement. I remember how he walked towards me that night to administer *'his justice'*, with a torch making horizontal lines in the dark. He had long strides and I could hear his shoes crushing on the path approaching me.

I couldn't run anywhere out of the house because it was too dark, and we didn't have any lighting other than the torch he was carrying to search for me. I gave up and sat there, to get what was served to me to let it pass, and he did. This was not just a one-off time, and we all embraced it as part of growing up.

Dad cared about his reputation, and he wanted to show the village that as a leader, his children were different; well-controlled and behaved. He took pride in all of us. His children were known from afar, and they still are.

All his three wives had to source food and feed their children and him. He was fond of beating Mum by inflicting hard blows to her

DAD

face and punches everywhere. Some days he would use big branches or simply a sturdy twig that would break due to the impact on her body.

Mum used different coping strategies like staying away on the farm, far from everyone else, or simply drinking local brew and keeping her feelings to herself because no one talked about how they felt.

One day, Dad came home before Mum, and he was drunk. He called for Mum, but she was not home yet. A few minutes later, Mum arrived but now, Dad had plans to discipline her. I heard Dad shut the door to his house and come over. I overheard him saying, *"Let me ask you, where have you been?"*

Florence, Gideon, Evans, Maureen and I were present; we were all under fifteen at the time. We were scared for her because we knew she was going to get beaten again. We all surrounded her saying, *"Mum, run!"*

Mum stood there helplessly because she had nowhere to run to and did not want to leave us.

Mum was also concerned about us seeing her getting beaten, but she couldn't do anything to stop him. He was walking very fast in long strides. We would flee in fear pleading with him to stop, to leave her alone, but he wouldn't.

Dad was like a monster when he was drunk and about to hit one of his family members, especially my mum or us, using his cowhide known as *'Bokora'*.

No one could stop him. He was tall and strong, and once he held your hand, you would have to wait until he was finished with you.

LOOKING BACK TO MOVE FORWARD

Instead of letting her go, despite her being so helpless, he grabbed both her hands, pulled her close to him and continued hitting Mum so hard that she fell to her knees.

At that point, I knew she needed help because she could not escape, although I didn't know how as I was only about eight years old – and tiny. I looked around and saw a rock that had fallen from the wall of our mud house. I picked it up and went to a corner of the house to hide; there was a short distance between us, but he did not see me because he was facing Mum.

Now, knowing how hard it is to tell your dad to stop his behaviour, to stop hurting your mum, it would take a lot of courage and I knew I'd be the next in line. I was not that good at throwing rocks or running. I aimed at him, prayed that it would get him. Luckily, it hit him hard on his abdomen. He stopped hitting Mum, shocked that a child had hit him for the first time. It was never heard of.

He looked around towards the direction where the rock had come from. He saw my younger brother Evans walking to help Mum, and he thought it was Evans who threw the rock at him. The next minute, Dad would spend it unleashing his anger on Evans saying to him, *"You will learn your lesson today to never hit me again."*

Evans was screaming in so much pain, so much so that I have continued to apologise to him to date. At least Mum got a reprieve. Although Mum stayed, she did not have to, but she had no alternative. Such experiences played a big role throughout my life in thinking about what I can do better to help women and children in such situations. The thought of a safe place has always lingered in my mind, but with no clear plan.

All my siblings used to get beaten by Dad for different reasons.

DAD

Maybe it was because we tripped and fell over, ran away when we needed to have our tooth pulled out, or vomited chloroquine after being forced to chew it before swallowing when we caught malaria due to its bitterness. Maybe it was because we lost or misplaced some animals that we were herding. Anything could land us in trouble.

He did not know how to be gentle, how to cuddle, or any words of affirmation because he had never heard any. It was always chaos and fear in our home.

Dad's name made us feel safe outside the home, but I felt scared inside our home.

One Sunday, it was my duty to herd the animals in a paddock far away from home. There was this boy who was employed to look after the animals briefly, however, Sundays were his days off. This day, he followed me from afar and I had no idea what he wanted from me. He would have been at least twice my age.

He approached from behind, fuelled by his intentions where he held me and started to wrestle me. There was no way I was able to get him off me since I was very skinny. I had to think quickly, and with the adrenaline kicking in, I was able to hold and bite his hand so hard. I heard him scream and threatened to hurt me badly if I did not let go of the bite.

When I didn't, he let go of me then I got a chance to escape. I ran away so fast that he could not catch me. He was not giving up and started to chase me from behind again, however this time I was aware, and I kept on running.

I shouted at him saying that if he came back at me, I would report him to Dad but if he left and never touched me, I would forgive him. He gave up. I could hear him breathing heavily from the wrestling and running. I was still going to report him, but I needed to use my brain to escape and get home safely because I was too exhausted to start the war again.

I got home with my clothes covered in dirt. Dad saw me, and he instantly knew that something bad had happened to me. He called out to me, *"Kagendo, come here, did he do anything?"*

I knew what Dad was asking. I said, *"No, I fought him off."*

The rest was history. Dad caught him by his hand and took over. I could hear the guy screaming from being beaten. Looking back, the vulnerability stood in front of us, where children get sent alone into the wild to herd animals with no adult in sight.

In my village, most men did not think of alternatives to approaching a dispute, other than physical altercations.

There was another time in primary school when my stepsister Faith and I trespassed through a man's farm to fetch water to bring back to school as a mandatory requirement. The guy saw us passing through his farm – which was a shortcut. Faith saw him, and she ran off. I was following her; I tripped and fell. The guy grabbed my legs and started rolling on me, beating me up.

He was one of the elders and we are not supposed to return a word as it's taboo, but I decided to fight him off because he was not going to leave me alone. I could not kick him hard enough to let me go using my skinny legs and I could not match his strength. Again, I had to use my teeth as my weapon, and I escaped after biting him hard.

DAD

When I got home and informed Dad, he went and gave him a stern warning that if he touches any of his children again, he will beat him. Although some people may call this trauma, we grew up thinking it was all part of growing up.

During his final days, I saw Dad trying to make amends by showing us that his heart was in the right place by being there for all his many children. I also learnt later that he did not want us girls to be irresponsible or get pregnant and drop out of school or get married in our pre-teens. I might have also been stubborn to counsel in my younger years.

For that reason, I forgive and thank him for protecting and encouraging us to attend school despite the hardships. He did not know any other way to approach and nurture us; perhaps that's the behaviour he had witnessed all his life, and for that, we do not resent him.

In Australia, I now realise this would be a police matter.

Chapter Six

MICHAEL

Mike is the firstborn from Mum's side. He is kind, inspirational, generous, smart and a beautiful human. As our firstborn, he has completed his job. Mike tried his hardest to live and set an example of a caring elder brother. Mike went through primary and secondary school as a top student always; he was younger than most of his classmates and shorter.

After finishing his high school studies, Mike carried the burden of a parent; just after he turned eighteen or just before. He attained good marks to qualify for government funding to get university admission. Before he could study for his degree, he had to serve in the National Youth Service.

Shortly after he started university, he also acquired work at a nearby high school where he could teach during university breaks to get

LOOKING BACK TO MOVE FORWARD

extra money. This is the money he would spare to pay for his siblings to ensure that we all went through high school.

For a sibling, I do not think many would outdo him for what he did for us, and I am yet to hear one. Mike would qualify as a hero in my eyes for changing our lives positively.

A hero for me is not just anyone who dives in to rescue someone, it is anyone who changes someone's life positively. He changed the lives of all his siblings. Mike believed in a fair chance that if a child is allowed to complete school, they would change their lives and that of the community and the world.

I did not see it at the time, but I got his point later, wholeheartedly. Although we did not have any pocket money at school to buy candy or anything else kids desire, Mike made sure that he paid for our

MICHAEL

tuition fees or communicated to the principals and gave approximate time to clear the fees debts.

He did not give up on the virtue of supporting his siblings. He stayed true to his thinking, without allowing distractions from lifestyle demands. Through his initiative, he started a small second-hand clothes shop on top of all the duties he had to get extra money to cover our fees. He had developed resilience from what he saw from our upbringing.

Mike was young when he took on all these responsibilities. Many people in his position could have chosen to follow their paths and forgotten their young siblings. I look at my other brothers and wonder how children from the same family with the same parents and hardships can have such different perspectives in life. I am glad that Mike was our eldest.

There were minor paths and issues we did not agree with Mike's reasoning at times, but now we are all old, we owe him more than gratitude. Mike knew that time was up and by looking around the village, he had a clear understanding of how we might end up if he looked in the other direction. He therefore, took a parent's role and he was aware that if he waited for our dad to pay our tuition fee, it would not happen.

Dad had exhausted his resources by educating our older halfsiblings and Mum had nothing, not even money to buy us food. Mike saw that Dad had retired from working in the police force, and his pension would not be sufficient to pay for our food or any other basic needs. It was non-existent.

I thank Mike so much for this opportunity. Not many people would do this much for their siblings, and this can be a lesson to us all to not give up on our families. Most people would move on with their lives once they get an opportunity to change their lives. Mike did not owe any of us his kind deeds.

As a young adult in university, Mike wore old second-hand clothes so that he could afford to pay for our important tuition fee. Mike worked hard, and he taught us by example. He was not lazy, he was not selfish, and he wanted good out of us all. He still does, cheering us on from the side lines. His insistent nature towards us to continue studying has seen us all acquiring qualifications that have set us free from poverty.

I wondered how special his brain worked to convince him to use all his savings to pay for our tuition fees. At times, he would go and teach for nothing, where the money he would have otherwise been paid went straight into our various school finance departments. The money he earned was split to ensure that Flo's, Gideon's, Evans', Maureen's and my tuition fees were cleared before the term ends. It was tough for him, but the best thing was that he had established this kind, sincere, personal and respectful relationship with the principals of these schools so that he could call and explain his situation and how he would work on his holidays to clear the fees.

They were inspired by his grit. They believed in him knowing that he was committed to ensuring that his siblings were not suspended from school due to unpaid fees. I thank them for their understanding because such brains are rare to find in the world we live in; those that foster initiative, positivity, and progress.

On many opening school days, we did not have all the required items on the list, however Mike ensured that he bought us the absolute basic items that were necessary like personal items and toiletries. We knew it was a struggle and did not demand anything. If Mike ignored us, we would have all fallen through the cracks, got early pregnancies and continued our dysfunctional lifestyle.

He was right because this is what happened to some of our close friends and neighbours. There were no strict government regulations to follow children through schools. They finished primary school but were not able to proceed to high school, ending up in early marriages not by choice. Some ended up in abusive marriages with young children and nowhere to return to after they left their homes.

When we all finished high school, it was time to proceed further. Mike spoke to us regularly regarding what we would be able to pursue in future, so we would not get distracted. We had to talk to him about the people we are inviting into our lives, while reminding us of where we come from. What we have endured and what we should make our lives look like before embarking on marriage and children.

Although Mike was hyper-vigilant, his insight guided us so that we do our best in making ourselves independent. He encouraged us not to wait for men to supply or meet our basic needs having witnessed our cultural norms.

I know he was right when I look back on our paths. We have learnt that hard work is a good virtue because there may be no other way to succeed or be able to be independent to buy what you want in life. Mike encouraged me to follow him to Australia where he invited me on a student visa, having paid my first term's tuition fee before I secured work to pay for the rest.

I wonder how many siblings would be able to stand by each other currently where resources are so stretched. When everything is about going ahead, paying mortgages and raising children. That peace begins from the home and then spreads across to the community and the world. We can be so full of ourselves with no intention to help, but we know that if you help your family or friend in need, it provides a huge relief, not only to them but to the community and the entire world.

Although we have branched out and made a life for ourselves in different countries, were it not for Mike, then we wouldn't be where we are. We say it takes a village to make an independent child. While we have not reached our peak yet, we have a solid foundation embedded that cannot be shaken. The dream is far from over because I believe that each one of us is unique and is destined for greatness – we just need to do the necessary work.

It stays with our story forever and this is what makes us who we are: unique beings. I am very privileged to witness the fruits of siblings helping each other and be able to tell it as it is to this day.

Chapter Seven

PRIMARY SCHOOL

All my siblings started at Marimanti Primary School, which sits in an extremely relegated part of Kenya where winters are not cold or windy, and summers are filled with dusty, dry conditions. The school is about 3km away from home. Sometimes, we could hear the bell from our home and children making noise during breaks or playing sports.

My first day of school was special, I had this cool uniform made from old clothes. It had pockets. Each morning of my *'Kindy'* (nursery), I would wake up, pour some water from a jerrycan into a basin and wash my face, hands and legs as it was a requirement to wash, then apply *Vaseline* if it was available. The uniform was touch and go for the lower primary school children. Not many children had shoes in my class; most of us were barefoot.

I was excited to be going to school each day. I would walk outside the compound and gather some wild fruits and stick them into my pocket for my snack later. Mum was away at the farm most of the mornings and we went to school on empty stomachs because there was no breakfast made for us – unless we had some leftover food from the previous night if we were lucky. This was our routine, and we did not expect it any other way.

Many a time, I thought about what survival meant to us as I grew up looking back. My question is, how did we live to see today? Here is why.

No one taught us to stay true to ourselves. We had to acquire the skills to empower ourselves. No one taught us resilience. We had to learn it from what we saw. Although our developmental and emotional needs were not totally met as children, we had to acquire emotional maturity with no entitlement, blame or dependence on anyone.

We had to keep the strength and our promise to ourselves to keep going, to power up the dream of being something. To everyone, to the village. We did not have shoes and white socks for photographs, we stood barefoot, always looking for food and safety. Grabbing and holding tight to what we found to keep us safe, for our own source of comfort, on top of conforming to societal norms and keeping up with the school obligations.

We had to be independent and arrange days and nights to suit the school requirements without input from our parents. We used to run flat to school each day because if we were late, we would be asked to kneel by the teacher on duty or the principal.

PRIMARY SCHOOL

We would then get a beating on the backs of our feet, calves or buttocks. I don't know which option was less painful or how any dignity was preserved by beating us, but it didn't matter at the time, so we just had to get to school on time...

The first lesson bell went at 7.30am and we would be finished school by 12.30pm for lower primary school and 4.30pm for upper classes. We would then walk back home – or run – because Dad knew the exact time when we should be arriving.

Walking to school barefoot in the morning was not too bad because it was still cool, however lunchtime was scorching with temperatures often hitting above 45 degrees. It was tough to navigate from school to home and back after lunch walking on hot ground and rocks. We ran from one tree shade to another to cool our feet. Not to mention harsh prickles, thorns and fierce creatures we had to dodge.

Classes were mostly full of dust, and we had to fetch water and pour it on the floor where we are sitting to settle the dust, water would evaporate quickly due to heat and wind and would set the ground to be intact until we ran and played on it to get the dust loose. The creek was a few kilometres away and the shortcut got me into trouble with the elder who beat me up for trespassing on his land!

We were also required to bring handheld sharp grass slashers and each evening, we would be required to slash the grass and weeds by hand during rainy seasons. It was also the pupils' job to repair classes and chairs if they broke or mud fell off. In some way, mending broken classrooms gave pupils some sense of responsibility and acquired life skills.

If we got a sum wrong, the teacher would ask us to hold our back of hands out and they would use a ruler to whack at the knuckles. We had to learn Kiswahili and English.

I was very skinny in primary school. There were two boys in my class who had nicknamed me a name that meant I would collapse if a breeze blew across or if anyone touched me with just one finger! The boys would corner me when there was no teacher around and whisper the name to me and leave. I feared them and I was not able to report or do anything because they threatened to beat me up if I reported them. I carried this name until I finished primary school. I never saw them since then, despite them being neighbours.

I heard that they did not make it past primary school. They got in all sorts of trouble with the law and one lost his life prematurely due to thuggery.

At school, there was a food program called *"Save the Children from Canada."* It was donors from Canada who changed pupils' lives with nutrition supplements. Most children were attracted to the school because of the food rather than the education part.

The food supplied was a packet of UHT milk for morning tea. For lunch, we would get boiled wheat or yellow maize with oil. Chickpeas were a luxury on some days. Later in the years, they were able to provide maize mixed with beans. If my boys landed here at this time, they would have starved due to their fussy behaviour!

To us, this was better than what we got at home, and enough of a nutrition supplement. For growing children, it was important to have a diet that provided us with a balanced diet besides filling our tummies. Some children also hardly ate anything at their homes

PRIMARY SCHOOL

besides whatever they could get at school and had to survive until they returned to school next day.

This sustained us for a while when Mum was away. Children used to line up and sing for these nice people who reassured us that there would be a meal the next day if we returned to school. And we did! I am so glad such kind people existed who changed the lives of many young children.

Most of those children have gone through education and supported their families because they returned to school the next day for a meal, and a packet of milk while the teachers sneaked in some learning! These are the kind gestures that seemed so minute yet made a big impact on so many children in my village.

We did not take these for granted and I wish such acts continued due to an ongoing need to transform the lives of many children.

Chapter Eight

SECONDARY SCHOOL

My siblings and I all went to boarding secondary schools, although it was costly. It was hard for a village girl to go to high school; there were no day schools in our area to attend to. We would stay at school for months before the mid-term break – but it was also convenient because we did not have to worry about travelling miles to and from school every day. It was almost an initiation by itself where you had to depend on yourself for all your needs, your self-care and teachers as your guardians.

I went to Chogoria Girls Boarding School and later my youngest sister, Maureen, also joined and completed her study two years after I graduated. Florence went to a different school, Mikinduri Girls, which sits about five hours' drive away in different direction located west of my village with no way of meeting mid-term. Gideon and Evans went to Chuka Boys school.

LOOKING BACK TO MOVE FORWARD

We had to wake up by at least three in the morning to walk to the local market to board an old land rover called *'Matatu'* which ferried people to the nearest connecting market. Here, we had to separate and join different vehicles which would take us in different directions towards our schools. There were plenty of vehicles once you got there compared to the one that we had to scramble for earlier in the morning – some people would miss seats and would have to sit on top of others or in rails with no guarantee of surviving an accident.

The trick to catching this vehicle that serviced the whole community in one trip was to get up early because there are so many other students and commuters travelling for the day. We would ride at dark, without seatbelts, and at times, muddy roads from the torrential rains or very dusty while stacked to the extent of sitting and breathing on strangers.

Rainy seasons were very tricky because of the roads and most of the time, the vehicle would get bogged and we had to get out and push it through the heavy mud – resulting in our shoes and school uniform getting covered in mud.

SECONDARY SCHOOL

After a five-hour trip, I would arrive at the township of Chogoria. I would walk uphill carrying a tin box with belongings to the school gate. Arriving at school in such a state made me feel ashamed looking at the other girls' spotless clothes and shoes.

Nonetheless, reporting to school on time was uncertain and depended on many factors for me and my siblings; Firstly, if there were fees for the term, uniform and essential and personal needs which mostly were a struggle. There was no money to pay for these, and girls' necessities like pads were unaffordable – not to mention sensitive if seen purchasing.

It was a wonderful opportunity to attend Chogoria Girls due to its good reputation. Chogoria Girls is a well-known school in the country with a good academic performance ranking at national level. It is particularly known for academic, drama and music festivals and other fun extracurricular activities.

To this day, it is run and guided by missionary values with high spiritual requirements through the Pentecostal church. The school was founded by Dr Clive Irvine, who was a missionary from the Presbyterian Church of Scotland in 1922, but it is now run by the Kenyan government.

The school sits about 4,100m above sea level which makes it freezing from June to August but most of the other months' temperatures are cold during the nights anyway. Although the weather was nice some days, we required jumpers and leg warmers most of the months. It was challenging for those who feel cold most – I can easily say I was one of the people who felt it most, given that my home location was always hot.

Prep studies were particularly challenging for me and made me somehow dislike this part of school routines because we had to be up at 4am to attend compulsory prep and later at night, which was mandatory. I couldn't learn in that cold, and it was stressful due to the pressure during those mornings. I used to pull my jumper sleeves, so they cover both my arms and my fingers, and I would then place my elbow on the desk to cover my ears and my face would be looking down at a book on my desk pretending to be studying but mostly asleep.

Not because I didn't like to study – I blame the cold. Teachers would find me dozing off and I would get in trouble. Other than a few hiccups, high school was fun for me, I made friends, and I enjoyed learning and having fun with other girls.

Chogoria Girls had its culture and attending church and seminars were mandatory during our time. There was a strict doctrine and ongoing culture of *'monolisation'* by older students. This is a word I understood as a newcomer to mean being initiated into high school life and bullying, without teachers' knowledge.

I learnt that the girls from the higher grades welcome the new ones to introduce them to girls' boarding school taboos to pass on the rituals that were forbidden and if any girl was caught practising, they would be suspended.

Like most teenagers, hormones were running wild. Furthermore, they were far from home and had no parents to hassle and restrict them. I think the behaviour of teenagers is almost at par with whatever part of the world you live in. The difference is the groundwork laid in one's childhood to be able to choose responsibly to match the values and expectations of a student. It was so troubling at times and hard to tame a group of very curious teenage girls.

The school knew about what the girls got up to and used paraffin oils in meals; a culture that was adopted by many institutions in a bid to tame the teenagers. There used to be Chogoria Boys School across from our school and we used to meet for church sermons and other extra curriculum activities.

Later in the second year of school after making several friends in my class, it was much easier to assimilate. Most girls got a chance to form friendships and relationships from the brother school. A lot of fun and mischief used to happen because some girls had mastered their skills. I was very naive and focused on practising what my Dad taught me – to stay away from the boys.

I would say I was inexperienced in most of the shenanigans and the furthest I went was receiving a cute letter from this boy, Richard, who kept sending them through a girl who met them frequently to talk to the boy she liked.

I would read them, and I replied once, which meant he kept writing more. Through the third year and the fourth, it was letters back and forth and in his last letter, he wrote that he would like to collect me from school on our last day. His idea was to take me to his uncle's house and spend the night *'watching movies'* then I would head home the next day.

I knew this would never happen because I was already too scared about the idea. For a village girl it was a big deal for me despite my classmates clapping at the idea and encouraging me to go.

When the last day of school arrived, my brother came to pick me up. I did not mention what was on my mind because he would have possibly found a branch somewhere and whacked me, then find this boy and whack him, and only once the branch was smashed, he would head home alone. I do not blame him.

I decided to seal my mouth and prayed that when we walk out of that gate, I would not meet Richard. We walked towards the gate with my tin box; in it was all my belongings. I was holding one side and my brother was holding the other side. Not too much to talk about, I was simply happy to be collected and heading home because I had to be signed off and picked up by an adult.

We went past the gate down the hill, and to my amazement, I saw Richard approaching us coming up the hill! There was no way I could look at him today, I thought. I spared myself and him a thorough beating. I had to look to the other side and pretend that I did not see him. Four years of waiting and nothing happened!

I knew how to relate better with girls because since childhood, I have never been caned or yelled at by my dad for walking along with a girl. In high school, I made a lasting friendship with a best friend Emma, we got along well. She comes from *Kisii*, and we speak a different mother tongue. For those who have learned about Africa or visited one of the countries, Kenya has about 40 different ethnic groups with different languages.

We spent most of our free time together and shared things after developing a close friendship. To date, we talk and laugh stupidly. We still remind each other of this night when she asked me to visit her cube which used to sleep only four girls because she was a prefect, while I shared my dormitory with over a hundred other students. It was a fun and exciting night. Children need to be allowed to be children, to be taught gently what is acceptable, what games can be played with boys and what is not safe. This way they can be autonomous and empowered to choose.

Growing up, there only used to be boys' games and girls' games, and if you were a girl seen in the company of boys, it sparked some

SECONDARY SCHOOL

nasty talks about you saying how misbehaved you were. No wonder this is what we grew up knowing. To fear boys instead of being taught how to successfully beat them in a sports game because this would be possible, without fear of shame.

Towards completion of high school, there was this trip that we were meant to pay for, so we could go to Mombasa – on the coast side of Kenya, around the Indian Ocean – for a week. Having come from the Eastern part of Kenya, I had never seen the ocean. This excursion trip would have been incredibly special to go with the other girls in my class.

Sadly, at the time, I was the only one from my class and one other student from another class who couldn't afford to go. We had to remain behind while my friends went away for a week because we owed tuition fees.

It was upsetting but I knew that clearing the tuition fee was more important and I did not blame my parents or my brother because I understood my situation. I vowed to myself that one day I will find my way to visit Mombasa once I finished school and found myself a job. I was not entitled, I had to understand that there were five of us in high school at my time and my brother had to pay tuition fees solely.

True to my word, years later, I visited Mombasa with my friend and it was an exciting experience.

Chapter Nine

NATIONAL YOUTH SERVICE

In Kenya, the parliament established the National Youth Service (NYS) around 1964 in a bid to train young people to be patriotic, reliant and disciplined. Those candidates who made it to the university up to the late '90s were often made to go through NYS. The government would pay part of their university fee whilst they served and built the country through a disciplined force.

NYS taught youth to be independent. It also made them tough and helped them understand that life was not easy out there. Depending on how the individual handled the experience, they could either stay at the college and finish their service time or just quit and make their parents pay for the university fee.

In my case, it was not because I was going through the university, and not because my parents made me go to NYS. After completing high school, I wanted to join a university to study for a nursing degree to serve and help my community after witnessing poor health outcomes in my area, growing up.

My applications to the universities were not successful. Firstly, my marks were not at the top grade for direct entry, and secondly, I was not financially stable (to speak directly) to offer a bribe in exchange for an admission letter. I also applied to some colleges to study a nursing degree or equivalent, but we were asked to forward a large amount of money to secure the application. We did not have the money at the time, so I missed that opportunity.

These practices still exist for most recruitment services and admissions to universities where they ask for substantial amounts of money from poor people. Unless you are a top student to access free education from public secondary schools and universities, most bright students will not go to the secondary school or universities of their choice due to such irregularities.

For that reason, I decided to join NYS to empower myself, my siblings, Mum and most importantly, many other women from my village who were told that NYS was for young men.

The NYS prepares most youth for all-around manual labour and access to some training for those who were interested in attaining diploma qualifications and further studies. They teach you drills and prepare you to work under pressure. The training is very intense where you go out of the camp for all-day hiking with no food or water in the worst conditions for almost no payment other than accessing some basic personal possessions for daily use and basic food. I knew this would be hard, but I had to get there to continue with my journey of finding a voice and strength to be a girl in my village. I knew it would be a gateway that I had to go past the training to secure a job to pay for all the required fees in the future to get where I wanted to be.

I knew I would be required to run fast to defeat my opponents to get this chance because I could not go back home and face my family with no admission letter in my hand. I knew that my medical exams would be okay. We had to pass for eyesight, teeth, HIV, and basic prerequisites like running which I knew I would pass – unless they pushed us aside for a bribe, for which I didn't have the money. I put my hope and my best foot forward because I wanted this badly.

I knew that opting for NYS would reduce all stress-related costs for my parents and my brother who had sacrificed so much. I knew I had to take it from here. My logic at the time was that joining NYS didn't replace my urge to join university to study nursing. I thought it would pave the way to future opportunities and buy me some time needed to mature, train hard and be tough to prepare for any kind of job that I had to find.

The recruitment day approached, and Dad insisted on accompanying me. This was the first time I felt that he actively engaged with me in a special and nurturing way, and he was really worried about me. I spoke to him at length about what it meant for me, as opposed to the teaching college that I did not want to attend.

I explained that he wouldn't have to worry about fees for NYS. We discussed it at length; he had some ideas of how hard it would be, having been a recruit himself and served as a police officer, he would have undergone thorough training in similar conditions during his time.

LOOKING BACK TO MOVE FORWARD

Dad wanted us to be tough, and brave to be able to face life head-on, so we can be independent. Whether it was the belting Mum and us or leaving us to fend for ourselves, his belief was we were responsible for our actions and the paths we take in life. But as a teen girl, seeing what Dad had done to Mum, it was so hard to forgive him and positively take his support. I feared him, so when he suggested that he was coming to support me during this recruitment, I refused initially but I couldn't negotiate with him, so I let him be. He knew why this was important for him, perhaps to make amends. I thought travelling far away from him would be safe for me because I do not have to fear him every day.

I had not given up hope that change was inevitable.

Dad was severely ill when I was undergoing the recruitment. He had liver and kidney diseases that made him fragile, and he could not engage in treatment due to inaccessibility and his nature of being tough. He could barely walk, he must have been in the final stage of his illness, having endured so much suffering quietly.

From a man so tall and strong to withering and becoming so weak that he had to use a walking stick to get around, it was hard to see the change.

On recruitment day, Dad was ready before I was. He grabbed his walking stick and followed me; he reminded me earlier about the time I had to arrive by so that I do not miss the opportunity. He used to have this gold watch that he never left his side; he wore it since I was a child. He also reminded me that I had to do my best to ensure my opponents don't beat me because I had a good opportunity to start my independence.

NATIONAL YOUTH SERVICE

I agreed, not frightened of him this time, but determined to make him proud. Dad wished me luck and off I went to the recruitment arena while he waited for me. He supported me through my cross country and clapped in joy when I took a second position. He was openly proud of me, and I felt so good seeing Dad smile at me in pure joy and pride for once in my whole life. That is when I knew that I could take a chance on myself to do it and that I would be okay.

I raced through this recruitment, cleared medically and was offered a place with one other girl both of us with no bribe. The other two failed, one in medicals and one came almost last in running but still got spots through bribes.

A month later, I travelled to Gilgil to embark on a training mission. The Gilgil training camp was so far from home where we underwent an exhaustive training for eight months. The training brew cruelty from most officers (not all).

After just two weeks into my training, things got hard. I did not hate the entire training experience, but I was secretly questioning why I joined. Firstly, Gilgil is very isolated and extremely far from home; the place is a 12-hour non-stop drive away. Hence, there was no way I could escape back if things got tough or even visit home on the weekend. Not that I missed home, and we were not permitted to visit before the completion.

Secondly, it sits in parts of Rift Valley province elevated to about 6,578ft above sea level. It got so cold, especially early mornings when we had to get up around 3am to get ready for the morning run around the camp singing *"Buffalo Soldier"*, among other songs.

Thirdly, the trainers were so loud. They yelled at the trainees and at times, I did not get the whole point of all that, but I later understood that the yelling was to transform and change recruits from their civilian coats.

There were heavy tasks that we signed up for. Gosh, I could not wait for the training to be over already! Most of the tasks were believed to be pure punishment and I had to keep trying to be hyper-vigilant to abide by the rules to finish the training. Some punishments included a frog jumping with a spade above your head, rolling on the hot concrete, being dipped into a mud pit and not being allowed to wash your face – let alone your body – until manna from above reigns.

Luckily, I always had clean shaven hair during my training; it helped with the mud pits. The cooks used to add kerosene oil to the food that was prepared for us with a belief that it would reduce the hormones and curb irresponsible behaviour from the recruits. You could taste kerosene from the rice blocks they made for lunch. Maybe it worked – maybe it didn't.

The drills and the physical training instructors make you dread your worth. Do not get me wrong, there were some good instructors and some fun training, but there were also tasking courses and horrible instructors that made everything seem so hard.

For example, one day this sergeant spat on my face for saying pardon. I could not believe it. I cried so hard, and part of the cry was that I knew I could wrestle her down, but I couldn't do it due to the consequences. I was angered inside and out; I wanted to quit and go home. I knew that this was a start of ongoing intimidation and bullying from her, that would never end unless I quit. I approached my house commander, Florence, and said that I wanted to quit and go home.

NATIONAL YOUTH SERVICE

Florence was mature and full of wisdom. She gave me a seat in her office and asked me to sit down. She knew that I was a good recruit and that something terrible must have happened. When I explained to her what had happened and that I wanted to go home, she said to me, *"Lillian, I know you. You are a good recruit, you will make it far because of your humility, but you can't quit yet. You can't cry when you get hurt, your mother isn't here, but I will deal with this because it was uncalled for."*

I thought to myself, what a champion. This is all that every girl needs, to not be scared or infuriated, girl needs a role model and someone to look up to, regardless of the situation.

Florence was incredibly supportive, reassuring and comforting, I felt empowered, and I wondered to myself if it was true that I hadn't done anything wrong. This behaviour is common for people with power where it gets misused.

After this conversation, Florence called out for this sergeant. I was asked to sit and watch it go down, and she delivered it for me. I listened in awe; Florence questioned her motive towards hurting me. I liked her idea of wanting to know what made her so furious to an extent of spitting on a recruit. Florence made sure that she got the answers as to why, and everything pointed out to this woman's temper. She was told that not only was it demeaning, but it was also embarrassing, and uncalled for and that it was not safe to spit at anyone given the dangers of transmitting diseases through one's saliva to another person.

Florence asked her to apologise and swore to me in front of her that if she did anything to me in future, she would get her dismissed from the service. The sergeant left and that was put to rest. I was fortunate to have someone who understood the situation and did

LOOKING BACK TO MOVE FORWARD

not side with the sergeant. Since then, she used to stare and shrug her shoulders but said nothing other than twisting her mouth in disgust.

Five months into my training, I learnt that Dad had become severely ill and had passed away. I had no means of travelling to his funeral. I felt a sense of loss, but I knew that Dad was at rest and free of pain. I knew he wanted me to power up to the end of the training and I was going to do as we had promised each other to complete and pave the way for future opportunities.

I had some responsibility to fulfil the promise and that is how I learnt to forgive him for those years of heartaches. I mourned Dad differently, and although my emotions were intense, I learnt to find comfort and distract myself during the training to avoid being overwhelmed. I knew there was no room for being carried away by emotions at this crucial time. I told myself, he was my dad, and luckily not my mother that I had lost, because the outcome would have been different.

In some ways, Mum and I got an eternal break from beating and fear. We did not take that freedom for granted. The rest of us are finding our feet again, with compassion and a heart full of forgiveness. It would have been great for him to witness what his children had become of late, but I am certain that he is watching over us and proud of our hard work that he was trying so hard to hearten.

Chapter Ten

PARAMILITARY TRAINING

After graduating from the NYS, I was fortunately recruited for paramilitary training before we were discharged back home. I was one of the lucky recruits to secure a spot which was by pure luck because some people didn't get a chance.

I knew my journey had gained momentum after my name was called out.

This time, Manyani training field was accommodative – luckily not so cold. I did not struggle this time and the training was so fun. Partly because I was now strong, healthy and fit after vigorous training at the NYS. But also, I had seen it all and prepared for the worst. I thought this was even better and it would open my way to the world, by being able to pay for my courses independently in the future to acquire the qualifications that I so desired.

I knew it was not going to be much different to what I had already experienced but I needed to give it my best to keep moving forward.

My motto was determination and not to give up if I wanted to change my path in life and opportunities. I drew strength from the positives that were awaiting me at the end of it, and it felt surreal and extraordinary to finally secure work. I also had friends from the NYS which made it fun and less threatening and felt familiar. We snuck out a couple of times to go and check out the nearest towns – thanks to a couple of my friends who were more courageous and adventurous. Although it was possibly risky, I was happy to try and be rebellious for a bit to see how it felt to not follow the rules.

We got caught the second time when one of the girls reported us which meant we had endless cleaning jobs in the mess hall and *so* many dishes.

Shooting in the range was daunting yet fun. It was a good chance to experience what our soldiers do on a day in the field of war. Stripping and cleaning of the riffles and assembling back while timed.

I was determined. I could not afford to make errors in the range, I came from far in the village and no accidents would be allowed here. I must admit that I did very well in shooting where I was one of the two females selected and placed in a line with men who were also sharpshooters.

We had a go at the G3 which was much preferable to aim at a target at 300m, however, the back kick was not desirable, compared to the FN choice which had a much smoother kick. I still own a registered

PARAMILITARY TRAINING

riffle, a Remington 223, which I take to the range occasionally and it feels good to smell that smoke out.

I tried my best without skiving my training and graduated. I was placed at a special unit based in Nairobi headquarters, but it meant we would drive to different bases and locations across the country. The special unit was mainly for the protection of forest resources which was great as the country has seen more positive changes in the utilisation of natural resources with protection around it.

I continue to be proud of the achievement of this organisation, which was a new establishment at the time and now thriving to achieve its targets in forest cover and protection.

One day during our patrols, we got a report on the radio about these criminals who had caused much havoc in the community and had stolen and caused massive tree destruction. A group of us was dispatched, and I was the only female to accompany the troop of men in a patrol vehicle. They were a great team to work with and I remember them making jokes.

We went to the site directed by the radio and cornered the guy. My mates were teasing me for an easy first offender to do whatever I wanted to do with him. With our AK-47, we approached him and now in handcuffs, he was pleading and not going to fight. I knew this guy had caused so much destruction and collaborated with some known criminals. I asked him why he was doing it, and he stared back at me.

He said that he had a wife and children to feed and educate. For that reason, I was convinced that this guy needed to run right now and find income elsewhere as opposed to any other punishment. I had to cut the rubbish but there was no way I could harm him.

LOOKING BACK TO MOVE FORWARD

All I said to him was, *"Get out of here and go find work elsewhere, you don't want to return because we will find you, and the outcome will be different."*

I understood whatever he had done, he was trying to fend for his family, and I trusted and hoped this was the case. With that, he ran off and we agreed that he had learnt his lesson unless he wanted to end up in jail next time, or in a worse situation, depending on the circumstances. The guy was very weak anyway, his strong mates had escaped and were not caught. We sent him with a word to spread and having been spared, he spread it.

After a year of proper employment, I started saving up some money. I bought Mum whichever dresses she wanted, a dining set and a patterned sofa. I sent her pocket money and bought her all the utensils she needed to cook for herself. Maureen and Evans, my youngest siblings were going through their last high school years, they had my support, and we were witnessing a major change in our lives in a better way.

It was a changing period to live and work in Nairobi, I even housed my immediate younger brother Gideon in my cube at the camp whilst he attended the University of Nairobi to complete his law degree. He is a very smart guy. He skipped a class in lower primary to catch up with me, and always beat me in class! Isn't that terrible? Gideon has completed his PhD and lives in South Africa working for UNHCR. He makes major decisions for the refugees' settlements. He has a wife and three beautiful girls and has continued to work hard to provide for his family.

These are just little things that have made a huge difference in our lives.

PARAMILITARY TRAINING

It is important to recognise that support and resilience bear some positive fruits and changes in one's life, but you must be willing to take the risks and do the work. I cannot imagine where we would all be if Mike didn't hold our hands in supporting and showing us the right way.

I funded myself to pursue a diploma and later a higher diploma in Human Resource Management. I graduated and took on a role as an officer in payroll. I was trained to use the Oracle program to process payments for over 4,000 employees.

To this day, I still find the knowledge useful in navigating life, colleagues and dealing with situations in general. This position saw me in the office more as opposed to the field. It was another proud achievement. I had to study part-time at night, because of the hurdle I stumbled upon after completing high school when I wanted to pursue my nursing degree. Nairobi is densely populated, and it was a hard commute at night.

I would use *'Matatu'*, which would stack us anywhere with no seatbelts – especially at night, but it didn't matter because it was important to get back home. One night, I witnessed a huge crash where a big vehicle had flattened about 10 pedestrians, I was at the end of the queue and had a near miss. It was scary.

Some days, I used to walk long distances and it was unsafe at night because there were no streetlights. This period also came with some challenges. One night, I started coughing blood and felt lightheaded. I had heard of a respiratory clinic located in one of the slum areas in Nairobi, which I visited one morning. To confirm my fears, I was informed that I had TB.

I remember thinking to myself, it had to be a combination of the commutes, the poorly ventilated small shack rooms where we were living called *'barracks'*, working in the HR office with volumes of clients' old, archived files covered in dust. All was not lost because it was treated and cured within nine months of continuous use of strong antibiotics.

Having gone past these challenges and passed, I felt empowered. I had a chance to contribute to better and help Mum. I thought it was my duty to look after her and guaranteed her that I would build her a better house one day to make her life comfortable in any way I could.

Three years after migration, I solely completed building Mum a five-bedroom three-bathroom brick-and-tile house which she now lives in, and we all use it when we visit. I felt that anything that I owned was for me to share with my family in a way that will make our lives better in moving forward as gratitude for what we had gone through.

Now, I do not have to hand them anything because when we held each other hands, we all took opportunities and worked hard to change our narratives and became independent. In my opinion, I've found that if you shared what you have in educating or supporting your sibling to have a sustainable job or college, you will be helping them to be independent including their children and they will leave you to enjoy your earnings in future.

For me, Mike set an example and Mum was and is still my rock. And although he's not with us anymore, I feel that Dad is already very proud of all his children. I have told Mum that our next project will be building the shelter for women and children that I have thought about since I was in high school. This will possibly be the last project I will do before feeling accomplished – if there is such a thing. But this project is remarkably close to my heart, and

PARAMILITARY TRAINING

I believe that what I have accomplished in the past is by far more challenging than this project.

In my youth, I helped my friend get her young son back from a highly dangerous ex-partner who had taken the child off her. We fled for over 300km to help her and her son hide. If this guy intercepted us or had known where we were hiding, I do not know what would have been the outcome. Her son has now gone through high school. Such a refuge would have played a crucial role in protecting her and her son at the time, and many other people I have heard their stories.

It may take me some time to build alone, but I will not give up. I have spoken to Mum severally about this project. Each time she questions how I will achieve this. My answer in my mother tongue has been, *"O ye, of little faith, I am strong, you are strong, we can start something small, and my children will finish when I grow weary."*

My answer has always been consistent. Mum likes my ambition and stubbornness. She has seen me purchase the first piece of land for this project many years ago and continued to add. Now she believes anything is possible, embracing the seriousness of, *"Yes we can."*

I have Mum's and sister's full support and local women willing to volunteer their spare time and wisdom of what would be beneficial in the community. Nothing has shifted from what I imagined it would look like many years ago, but after living in Australia, I understand even more what would truly be needed and beneficial for women fleeing for their safety.

We hear stories of helpless victims staying in toxic relationships even when it is not safe to do so because they do not have anywhere to run to – just like what my mum and many other women continue to do.

LOOKING BACK TO MOVE FORWARD

We must believe in change.

There are so many untold stories in my village that go unheard, or women would like to speak up but keep quiet, due to fear for their lives. Inequality towards women continues among the dominant gender in most parts of the world. There are limited resources to empower our women to stand up for themselves and choose what is good for them. People who are seen as activists continue to be assaulted and killed.

Kenya does not prioritise women in the village or parliament or any positions of power which is sad. Just in Kenya alone for example in a community far from my village, a report organised by *Homa Bay County Government* in 2020 and carried out by the *Overseas Development Institute* and *LVCT Health*, with support from *UNICEF* found that gender inequality, poverty and difficulties in accessing services are fuelling high rates of unintended pregnancies and HIV in a small region of Western Kenya.

It was uncovered that adolescent girls are at risk of sexual violence which increases their risk of acquiring HIV and inadvertent pregnancies in this part of the country. Violence and sexual abuse of underage girls continue to be unreported due to fears of stigma and prejudice or fear of retaliation from the wider community.

The report highlights that one third (33%) of adolescent girls aged 15 to 19 in Homa Bay are mothers or pregnant with their first child – almost twice the national average of 18%. It also shows that youth aged 15-24 contribute 13% of the total number of HIV infections amongst 15 to 49-year-old in the county, with almost similar trends in other parts of Kenya.

This is rarely heard of in Western countries where health care and the protection of human rights are prioritised. *(Action urged on*

PARAMILITARY TRAINING

teenage pregnancy and HIV, as a new report reveals high rates in Homa Bay (unicef.org)

My hope and that of others are that efforts on the campaign and actions for curbing HIV and AIDS-related infections among adolescent girls and young women as a public threat by 2030 succeeds. Not just for Kenya, but globally.

I can only imagine the devastation of the parents of these young girls and what they may be going through – surely no one deserves that. It is hard to fully grasp the impact these issues, especially if someone has not travelled and seen the devastation on these children's faces, not to mention their parents.

HIV is a ticking bomb. Such narratives sit hard on me, hence the need to spread awareness and foster safe spaces for young girls to escape such acts of violence to empower them in future. Karibu Women's Shelter will focus on empowering the victims and spreading such awareness while protecting women and children's rights.

Chapter Eleven

WOMEN

Women do their best because when you are born a woman, the duel starts. It goes non-stop and we navigate all systems in life at full steam. For those who know, we are quiet warriors, we fall and get back up.

Whether it's through supporting your child struggling with a disability, or our life cycles with hormones, and life tribulations, these make us who we are, and they are the colours in the pages of our lives.

I embrace my life experiences as important in making me a grown woman. I feel happy when I hear about a successful woman's story. A strong woman who manages to go through setbacks to build their resilience into someone they want to be. I just think it is brilliant and I am left in awe of how they have gotten there, knowing full well that no one has it easy to get where they want to be.

LOOKING BACK TO MOVE FORWARD

At times, it is nerve-racking and sometimes it takes so much emotional and physical toil on one's life – not forgetting the sacrifices made along the way.

Whatever their narrative, their story and their beginnings are, they have done their best, and that is what is important. They did not wait for it to be handed over to them. I have seen women getting back to adult studies or taking on job challenges after raising their children, and it is tough especially if they had time off to have the children.

The reason behind such is what is important to them, to empower themselves. Women go through barbed wires to get past the boundaries of bullying, misogyny and mistreatment.

There are those women who continue to help other women to feel empowered by holding their hand to pass a hurdle, supporting them at work to get past a conflict, or mistreatment or showing courage in whatever field of representation they hold.

WOMEN

Your efforts are acknowledged, and young girls, women, even boys, and men, look up to you for courage and determination – those who can draw it from your experiences and lessons. Offer them a gift of hope and inspiration. Share it with them and you will be their hero in their own way.

Let them know that one day they will go past tough times knowing that others have walked similar paths and have made it.

Let us all give what we can, whether advice or emotional support, as these play a key role in growing women and for me; it has helped shape my journey in many ways.

Women give back to their communities by being who they are and in diverse ways, not because they have plenty, but because they have looked back and wished someone helped to unlock their paths earlier or told them that they are valued. They want to inspire other girls to get out and make a better life for themselves. To inspire them to have a voice. Giving to let out the urge to eradicate scarcity, emptiness and lacking.

Their hope is abundance and efficiency.

I see my female colleagues working so hard to just complete their tasks before they go on a week's leave because they do not want to think about it at night when they are sailing somewhere miles away. They do not want to task their colleagues who already have massive workloads.

Women remain true to their grown-up children and house them because they know it is tough out there for their daughters with their grandchildren to keep it straight due to mental health issues and domestic violence. The list is endless because we have all seen them in action, and we applaud you for that. If you can help in any way, please do.

All I see in women is determination, resilience and genuine drive with not enough words to utter out here that would reflect my adequate admiration. I say to any child out there; listen and respect your mum, she has gone through a lot to get you where you are. Learn and help your dad to look after your mum because she won't be there forever.

With your parents' love and guidance, you can study and achieve your heart's desires, but you must put in the hard work. My thoughts about a rocky childhood and upbringing, to tough life challenges, are well acknowledged as part of my journey from Kenya and after migration because they are a part of me.

To navigate life, to live and work with different kinds of people from all walks of life, you've got to appreciate what you went through and what you learnt from your tough experiences.

No amount is enough to equip us with the tricky situations ahead – especially as an immigrant living in a western country. Women uplift others by supporting them, not speaking behind their backs with rumours that they can't validate.

Not to say that there is any gender that does not deserve praise. It does not mean that men are not important or do not put in adequate effort.

Some men have remained strong pillars for their families, kudos to you. Others have taken enough responsibilities, to care for, nurture, and bring up children amidst all their life challenges. Some men have a genuine interest to be involved in their children's lives but have lost custody. They provide financial and emotional support whilst performing home chores. It is when such duties don't get fulfilled or aligned that chaos starts.

I heard a while ago that the man is the head of the home, while the woman is the neck that helps the man to turn around to face and traverse the right path. I thought it matched their description. That means both parties should work in harmony to achieve family goals and be reciprocal in building a community.

On the other hand, some men do not necessarily treat women as their necks, I have seen it. There are many 'heads' who do not place any value on their necks leading to poor coordination and chaos. Most men from my village would fit this description. Luckily, most women have continued to open their eyes widely, while men's evolution continues – although there are still challenges that continue to face women back home and other parts of the world due to a lack of financial independence.

The challenge is that women cannot just run away if things aren't going well, and despite the devastation, most women continue to get stuck in situations that are uncomfortable and disheartening. That is my observation and not all men would fit into this basket, because I have seen and heard about wonderful men too, especially in Australia.

In my culture, most men continue to look down on women, without placing any importance on their existence. It is hard to blame them or try to challenge their beliefs because they have never seen any different. Their belief about how to treat women might have started from their childhood. It would take a village to convince these men to look at the bigger picture. This is the change that men must embrace to see good in women and not just objects.

LOOKING BACK TO MOVE FORWARD

I have also seen something questionable after migrating to Australia and interacting with some men who have a slightly distinct perspective, which I will leave out for now and hope for ongoing evolution in their paths.

For most men I come across these days, I am happy to give credit to their efforts and support at home, where most roles are shared. Luckily, women who are hanging around them have dignity and a substantial career and some independence. This is a great empowerment for women to have something they can hang on to if things don't go well. I noted that there is a vast number of working women in Australia, who bring home as much income as their male partners. Some bring even more home, which is a big step ahead to women's empowerment compared to back home.

The elders say that it takes a village to raise a child. A village back home is important in keeping an eye on the children. It is important to note that the roles of both partners working and raising children in this fast-paced and busy life are challenging and may need to be negotiated with each home to suit their needs and routines.

For example, I found that it was helpful, and it saved costs for partners to start work at slightly different times for school drop off and pickups. Meal preparations and cleaning up can be shared and not just a woman's only job – most working couples again have adopted a system that suits them.

As an immigrant with no extended family abroad, it was challenging to work full-time and raise children due to the physical and mental exhaustion resulting from work demands.

For someone working in health care or any busy work environment with children, their duties never stop. Some days, after finishing work and

WOMEN

picking up children from after school care, the work doubles. I know many women who are going through such or even tougher conditions.

It is even harder for single parents to run the home and navigate the systems to ensure children are supported at school to feel safe to learn and regulate emotionally. Women run on low, hormones plunge, they forget their self-care to run around and support their children and their husband.

In my observation, I must say that despite the part of the world you come from, most men claim their place in their narrative. These sorts of men's perceptions of their world and others they live with including interactions may be in total dismay.

Women need empowerment by helping them to have a voice, although I recognise this can be too traumatic when they do not have anywhere to run to for safety. Most women try their best to serve and please their male counterparts to gain stability; I have seen different perspectives.

What happens when women can't run away and must stay in the same abusive situations due to fear of being followed and harmed if they escaped?

Is there always someone to help to hold their hand and link them up with the right services each time?

Over minding my business and being a kind neighbour who does not bother anyone, I had a weird experience in Australia that confused me. I once lived near a middle-aged couple and the man had a few odd behaviours that stood out. He would stand on the corner of his fence and mine motionless looking straight over to my kitchen window, and as soon as I looked outside, he would run off.

LOOKING BACK TO MOVE FORWARD

He placed a chair on top of his trampoline and a ladder over the fence overlooking my house where he would stare at us sometimes. I was confused about how to associate with him as a neighbour.

Such and many other odd behaviours continued to occur whilst I thought he was busy doing his business in his yard. Although this would be considered mild by some, it was a bit troubling when you hear kids saying, "*That's creepy,*" nicknaming him a meerkat as he sneakily, constantly stared at us.

One morning, I heard him hurling insults at his partner and possibly beating her. I do not like to judge anyone, but this just confirmed his behaviour that he did not respect himself, his partner, women or the child that he was raising.

Whatever the issue that had gone wrong, it was clear from his language that he was one of those men who care more about themselves than the rest of his family. Landing myself a neighbour with such behaviours was unfortunate.

No parent wants to give their beloved daughter away and then hear that she is getting beaten by their partner because she was too tired to clean up the dishes. She was possibly woken up several times at night to tend to the baby while he slept.

No brother wants to see their sister bruised by a man who has an ego and an inability to direct his anger elsewhere.

No child wants to hear it all or see their mother getting harmed by the man they call Dad.

After enduring this behaviour for a while, I went to their home with intent to speak to his partner. The guy saw me and came to join us, insisting to know what the matter was. We had already exchanged numbers with the partner, and I thought he should hear it from me. I raised my concerns and left because he was getting increasingly violent. I later offered to support the lady in future should she need help. She was shocked but amazed by my courage to speak out, she thanked me.

Although I was also scared of him, he stopped his lurking behaviour behind our yard for a while, and we learned that it was best to ignore him.

I have lived around great neighbours which is wonderful, but it gets challenging and my advice for any man is to look after women in their lives because when you get your man flu, she will be the one running around making sure that you get better. I know most men are tough, however, others turn into a *'pork chop'* from just a cough (Australian slang that I learnt years ago from my friend Vanessa to mean sulkiness). This is when men become sick and bedridden in their deathbeds for days, weeks, even months, of this awful illness, on and off. They cough thunder and scream lightning in pain, and women must acknowledge, validate and treat them with utmost care.

In my childhood, I did not see a sick parent. Not a single day I saw my Mum sick – even when she was, she hid it. She never rested because of a painful knee or headache, even now with arthritis crippling her, with a few falls due to her legs giving up. She gets up and goes even when the pain is excruciating. She is still tilling her local farm, despite having options to pay people to do this for her, she likes to keep active by growing her vegetables.

This is the narrative for many people in my village. Dad never mentioned illness all his life until he was sick with the liver disease that took his life.

LOOKING BACK TO MOVE FORWARD

Women are doing enough for their families and the entire world, sometimes they feel tired of being resilient. They just want to drop everything and breathe with ease due to exhaustion. A woman wants softness, a sense of relief, care and appreciation. She wants to spend and enjoy time with her kin as opposed to the rush and madness that is never-ending.

As a woman rights advocate, my insight is to all men out there who look at women doing it tough and fail to recognise and support them. Go out of your way and acknowledge a diligent woman because they know why they are doing it. They know the song and cycle they want to change. Whether they have reached there or not, just encourage them to keep reaching for what they believe in.

My experience as a mother of young babies was harder when I had to return to work after they turned six months. I also found that after speaking to women in the playgroup that they were all having the same feelings of genuine heartbreak. They have had to express their breasts at work and stored their milk in work fridges. They are at work physically but mentally and spiritually they are thinking about their babies.

Not to mention, as soon as they think about their babies, the milk starts trickling. This experience is hard on both the babies and mothers – although they do this for independence, to provide for their family and contribute towards their community.

Women who have undergone this, I know the feeling and I could count several times when I felt like my spirit had left work to go and comfort and settle them the first few weeks until I got used to this discomfort.

WOMEN

Days used to be long, and I could not wait to go home to cuddle them after work. I wished there were other possible measures and different outcomes for women to have an extended leave with some form of support to not have to rush back to work prematurely – perhaps a gradual return with some form of support, with more supports for single parents.

It would be helpful if they were given the opportunity or choice to ensure parents stay at home with their babies for the first year without being financially disadvantaged. It is very unsettling for children – no wonder we have so many children here struggling with attachment issues, anxiety and other diagnoses.

Perhaps offering family-friendly workstations and encouraging work-supported daycare centres where mothers can have a quick break to comfort their children might help them to transition smoothly. I think it would be a great outcome in terms of productivity.

I am hoping the more women get ahead the more discussions and opportunities to implement change to even pay gaps to foster financial security and equality at all levels to recognise the hard work the women do.

During my return to work after maternity leave whilst the babies were still little, I had some questions regarding how safe the babies would be. I guess such questions go through every mother's head, especially first-time parents. For example, I questioned how safe our babies were at day care without their parents – especially if they cannot talk and were not able to tell their parents about their day when they get picked up.

I did not doubt the care they received one bit, but I was not okay. Most of the time after I dropped them off, I would hop back to the car and cry. I questioned if this is what being a working mother in Australia was like. I was desperate to continue working but also be a mother, and I felt like I lost my identity.

Although I continued to leave my children at day care centres, I was severely torn between what was important in life. The thoughts constantly kept telling me that it was cruel for my children to be lost all day without me with a stranger in the first year of their lives. I thought to myself several times, was it more important to go and support other people while I *'dumped'* my children and paid money to strangers?

Nonetheless, I trusted the Australian system. Overall, when a woman is pushed with no choice, she will do whatever it takes to fend for, raise and protect her children. Ultimately, she is prepared to face such challenges because obtaining work is a gateway for a woman's independence.

Those women who have been talking for years about change and how women should be treated are well known and it would be great if they were included in contributions towards change that we all hanker for. There might be a possibility that once the great countries take charge in implementing such important change, then the rest of the world, including African countries that mostly draw their policies from Western countries, may adopt to change.

Recognise women as they bear fruits of standing up together and building a world where we can all enjoy the resources and support one another looking after the environment that provides us with food.

Back home, women are focused on supporting their husbands who want to further their studies whilst they stayed at home to look after the home and cook for them and their children. Some women result to being mistreated soon after their men finish studying and are earning enough money to find a younger and better-looking lady.

The older one may not be treated as important anymore. Here, women do not get a say but listen. These women are strong and seem to understand that it is not okay yet when trying to bring it up to move ahead, they get shunned. This cycle is repeated in many families and stories are different with each family unit.

Growing up, women's education was not important, and only education about a women's value, role and expectation in society was fostered when young girls were subjected to Female Genital Mutilation (FGM). It is what happened to us girls and continues to happen in the village, there may be little changes with time.

FGM is by far a traumatic experience for any young girl undergoing it. The common age group in my village to be subjected to this practice is girls between the ages of eight to 15. I underwent this at 13 years old; my younger sister was only nine years old. The experience is made to look like a celebration, but it is not, it is frightening however, the girl may not have the knowledge or choice to avoid this awful practice, unless she comes from a well-informed family.

On the day, the girl is asked to nominate a sponsor who is someone known by the family and has undergone this process herself. The sponsor's duties will be looking after the girl until she heals. The sponsor puts a mat at the entrance door and sits waiting for the girl.

Women form a barricade blocking the view past the circle.

Once the circumciser is standing on the door with a small knife or mini axe signals, the girl is supposed to jump and sit on the sponsor's lap with her legs apart, hands clenched in a fist staring blankly at the sky without blinking to signify bravery.

The circumciser bends and cuts the flesh a few times then she screams to signal completion and the flesh is thrown into the dirt. The blood is also left to leak onto the ground, where some dirt is sprinkled on.

There is a series of songs that follow while women are checking to ensure the cut has been done as traditionally. If satisfied, they wail in joy, but if not satisfied, the cut is repeated. It is not a nice experience. Once completed, the girl is asked to walk back to bed and lay on her back for weeks until the wound heals.

If the girl flinches or blinks during this practice, she will be nicknamed a mean name and will be spoken about in the village, spreading shame to the girl and the family which is not a nice experience.

She will lose her friends because no peers will want to be around a coward. By far it is a painful and a competitive experience by the teens to secure friendships in the village. There were no anaesthetics or antibiotics; just raw cuts on their parts and left for weeks to heal, staring up on trusses with their legs apart protecting the delicate wound from being knocked to cause fresh bleeding or infection.

When isolated to recover, the older women spoke to the girls about how to obey and respect men. Girls were taught what they are, how to sit with their legs crossed, to wear long dresses, and how to look after their men. There was no teaching on how a girl can be anything like a leader or defend their rights as a woman, how they carry themselves and do their studies or simple education like interacting with boys without being shunned.

WOMEN

This practice is still ongoing in many African countries and continues to impact women, especially during childbirth and other limitations. There have been some efforts to stop this practice and I am hoping to spread awareness to stop this from happening to young girls.

Back home, I saw nothing was there for you if you are a woman. I have seen brothers fighting their sisters for inheritance because women are not supposed to be counted as heirs. Women in my village are meant to serve as resting places where husbands use them to rest their hands by beating them so hard, like punching bags.

That is what I saw at home and knew growing up in my village as normal.

Women are supposed to do all the hard work on the farm, feed children and their husbands, graze animals, and pretend they are happily married, but they are illiterate. They are forced to think that they have no future and that their husbands are the kings of their homes and must obey them. Women are supposed to feel guilty when children go hungry or sleep rough, it is not men's duty to think that hard.

I draw and reflect on how hard I work, an expectation that was engrained from my childhood, non-stop to provide for my kids. I do not like uncertainty. I do not say, *"Whatever will be will be"*, as most people would say.

Like many other women, I like to be in control for some security and certainty. Women back home are well-controlled emotionally and physically. They are reminded and made to believe that they cannot live without their husbands. Some women have said that their ex-husbands continued to gaslight them and instil fear by saying to them that they cannot live without them to function in society.

LOOKING BACK TO MOVE FORWARD

For some women, it may seem true – especially those who never got an opportunity to study, be independent or have anywhere to run to. They are the ones running the household to provide for everyone. No questions for the husband despite being out the whole day and returning home late with no food but demanding their conjugal rights from women. If a woman questions, they get beaten up, if they return to their parents, men follow them there and beat them up in front of their parents then return them home, or their brothers beat them up and send them their way.

In my journey, I have wept for women and in the past, I have wished to trade some of the women's places to save them from the physical and emotional turmoil. I have seen hardships to the core.

This is where I draw my empathy for all women, irrespective of their background. We are all beautiful and we deserve respect and nurturing because we have made this world what it is today.

If the beliefs and attitudes towards women are positively fostered, then we will achieve unachievable. These bodies carried our children, for those who were privileged to be mothers. Our bodies carry our souls therefore we need to worship them. Beyoncé once said, *"Girls run the world"* because it is true.

Girls need to feel empowered and supported in all walks of life to achieve their pinnacle.

This is the perspective I am drawing on, hence the inspiration to start a small initiative for the local unheard women. I have seen Mum's face, and the faces of other women and their children in fear, hunger and anguish. I cannot run away from that what is stored in my memory of what I have seen unless I do something about it; that is when I will find peace.

WOMEN

To give them a choice to run away with their children to a safe place where they can have a shower, a meal and look after their children, educate them or have a trade to be independent. I want to build a women's shelter in my village because I have seen it all first-hand.

I know I won't rescue everyone in the village but whatever small impact I make I will be happy and proud to have started something that will help someone else. I have never heard of any women's shelter in Kenya because it is insignificant to the leaders in our community. No one has been strong or brave enough to start this kind of initiative, despite how important it would be to help women and children because of the growing need.

We can start something that will make a huge difference in creating opportunities for these women and unfortunate children.

Imagine putting a smile on a woman's or a child's face who did not feel like they had a purpose in life. I want to gift them that.

Chapter Twelve

ADULT LIFE AND MIGRATION FROM KENYA

It takes determination to look past the hurdles and think of how change can happen for the better. We can keep talking about wanting to change our situations but if you want that change to happen, you must choose a different path and do the work. If you sit in the comfort of where you are regardless of the discomfort, nothing will change.

LOOKING BACK TO MOVE FORWARD

Sometimes it helps to have someone in our lives whom we can have an honest discussion to point us in the right direction regardless of the rawness of the truth because it may feel overwhelming and confusing. Other times, this option is not there, and you just must go with your intuition, and hope for the best.

For me, Mike was there to shine a light in such moments. Firstly, he helped me end a failed relationship with this guy from the army who was my first boyfriend and was very violent, having known each other from the NYS. Later after meeting each other's parents like our tradition, I did not have any say moving forward because I was a woman. I would be required to cook for him, boil his water for showering, and do everything else a girlfriend was supposed to do.

One day after cooking him lunch at my cubicle, a text message came to my phone, and I went to read it. The guy grabbed my phone to check the message which I didn't like, and I asked for my phone. This started a huge fight and a WWE wrestling match almost like those I had watched in the '90s on a black and white television. Ultimately when I couldn't let go, he threw me across the bed and bit me so hard under my belly button, declaring him the winner of the match!

A lot of thoughts went through my head, and I got so scared of him. It felt like a chunk of flesh had come out of my belly due to the pain and amount of blood gashing out. I let go of the damn phone before he killed me. He was disappointed after reading the message that Mike had sent me saying that he had found a university admission for me, and he needed me to start the visa application process. The guy threw my phone at me and stormed out, leaving me scared of his next move. His bite left a mark under my belly button that is still visible.

ADULT LIFE AND MIGRATION FROM KENYA

After this event, I spoke to Mike regularly who continued to empower me to end this disastrous relationship. I knew that I was lucky to have a supportive brother and that I should take his offer seriously. The incident was not the only one that confused me and made me realise life can be lost in a heartbeat and need to learn lessons from the past and power up.

Weeks after this break-up, one very early morning on May 27th, 2007, a fire engulfed our shack barracks in a matter of minutes.

The previous night, we had watched the Armageddon movie with one of my close colleagues in her cubicle. I thought it was a good movie. My friend and I were in good spirits when the movie finished, we bided each other goodnight and I walked back to my room.

The next early morning, I left to have a shower outside the toilet pit that we used to shower in. It was a dark, cold winter morning in Nairobi. By the time I returned, there was a fire sweeping through our wooden barracks.

The barracks were made from plywood and iron sheets that fuelled the fire to consume everything. I had only a t-shirt and a towel below that I wore to the shower.

Amidst the confusion, I ran around to help others out and get a few belongings knowing it was not safe. I ended up sustaining some burns to my right arm, with scars visible as a reminder of a life almost lost.

The barracks were consumed leaving us homeless, but it did not matter because everyone was safe in the end.

I can now smell smoke from far away and I get hyper-aware and alert. I knew this was a near miss but I'm lucky to be alive – perhaps signs to put more thought and belief into migrating to Australia. It was another learning journey that I embraced as a reminder that I had a chance to walk a different path to change my life. Mike spoke to me about opportunities that awaited if I put more thought into our conversations.

I imagined high-rises and soil that didn't stain clothes. I imagined how most people on the streets will be white and how will I feel standing out… Would I be safe?

Despite feeling excited about starting this journey, I also felt the uncertainty of the unknown. But in all, I thought that Australia was different given the first occupants of the land were Indigenous. I heard Australian people were lovely and I choose to keep that in my mind until proven otherwise with a view that this opportunity will help me change Mum's life for the better. She will have some buttressing to know that she did it for us for those years and now we are paying her off. That she has raised a girl who has tried hard to help reverse the cycle of dysfunction.

When you live in a country like Kenya, a mention of migration to a Western country is a ticket to 'greener pastures', as my friends would say. For me, it would mean a better life with adequate opportunities, and a safe place to live, raise and educate children. All that we lacked in life. It would mean that my children would have more opportunities than we did to pursue whatever they desire to achieve.

Migration meant that I would be able to study nursing and save funds to bring my mother and other siblings if they wished to follow me to help them achieve their dreams. I thought of freedom where people could walk day and night in cities without the worry of their handbags getting snatched. I thought of the possibility of owning a car, house and anything else we missed out on growing

ADULT LIFE AND MIGRATION FROM KENYA

up. It also meant that I would be able to save up and buy a parcel of land to start the initiative of the women's and children's shelter to give back to my community, a cause that I yearned for.

Flooded with these ideas, I had to quickly start the visa application paperwork. First was the driver's license training, Yellow Fever and Hep B periodic vaccinations, then it was the IELTS English tests, then the medicals that took a long period to complete. This whole process took about a year for me and by the last day of 2008, I landed at Brisbane airport after a 24-hour journey with a stopover at Dubai and later in Singapore.

It was my first time flying, and I must say it was intriguing. The jet lag was immeasurable to experience for the first time. It was a stinking hot and humid summer in Australia, and my body was feeling a bit overwhelmed. The sun also seemed brighter, and the glare was unbearable, perhaps due to the long trip and the jet lag.

From Brisbane, I boarded a domestic *Qantas* plane to Rockhampton. I discovered the land *"Down Under"* as described by the *Men at Work*. I thought it was a long way away from home. Everyone wants to come here to explore and taste a *Vegemite* sandwich that we heard about growing up.

On my flight to Rocky, I discovered how picturesque and interesting it was looking down the ocean and the land. I even grabbed a magazine where I first learnt of Ellen DeGeneres and Portia, and I thought to myself how lucky these women were to be accepted by the world.

During this flight to Rockhampton, I also had a little think about the world in general and I wondered if a time would come when everyone in the world will have such freedom from discrimination, and judgement and live a free life as one. I reflected on our culture and how closed off from the world is and felt pity and concern.

We arrived at Rockhampton Airport where Mike and his family were waiting for me. Mike drove us back home, with nursery rhymes playing in his car for his four-year-old daughter Alycia-Jayde whom I met for the first time.

It took about two days for my head to adjust and feel right. The heat continued and sweat would break from just being in the house with windows open. I had never used air-conditioning before, and I was used to sitting under a tree or shade for a breeze. The solution I thought was to have numerous cold showers but every time I stepped out of the shower to dry myself, I would sweat again. I wondered if this was the life I had chosen, but I thought that my body will get used to it.

It got better after a few months. I knew it was a big move and a new life awaits, I just needed to bury my head deep in the sand to think about how to get ahead. My thinking and awareness had to change to adjust to the current environment with new cultural differences. I was also pleased to know that I am among these privileged people I see around, who have been born here, but now I have an opportunity to catch up.

I looked around the suburb during my walks and I wondered why some white people were poor and were on the streets begging yet they lived in this country. I also saw teenagers sitting under one of the bridges passing cans that had alcohol inside. I was confused as to why they made bad choices to not take this accessible education to be what they want to be – as the *CQU* motto read.

ADULT LIFE AND MIGRATION FROM KENYA

I asked myself what responsibilities would a teenage child have after completing school in this country that took their priority to study and qualify before maturity? I knew that it was neither my business nor the reason why I came here. I had work to do without forgetting where I come from.

I walked past looking the other direction not to stir them up.

Whatever the reasons were to the endless questions that I had, none got answered. I was too naive to ask a random person about my curiosity regarding their life choices. I was not going to judge because it was part of my awareness. I was not there yet.

I thought to myself that one day I may be able to get the courage to talk to young people regarding these opportunities they take for granted. I also thought that I may be able to help people struggling with life situations to understand that their tricky life experiences do not define them.

Chapter Thirteen

UNIVERSITY

I was enrolled at the CQU which sits in Rockhampton, a regional part of Queensland, Australia. I was told that the city is the beef capital of Australia, and it did not disappoint with the steaks!

I enjoyed living in Rockhampton as a new place because everything was handy and easy to get from one place to another with less traffic and free parking, especially having come from a village. It was not a big city to navigate compared to Nairobi – and the roads were immaculate. The gardens were maintained and there was no litter on the road or the parks.

I thought Australia was amazing. We had to pay for water but then this was all connected in the showers and kitchen sinks which I had not seen back home, let alone dishwashers and laundry facilities – so luxurious I thought. Almost everything was done with machines instead of manually. I saw lawnmowers instead of hand slashers. Girls' and women's hands were soft with no blisters and calluses from hand labour. The bins were emptied by a loud truck that used to wake me up every Tuesday morning.

There were many other differences I found as I navigated the first few months. The fruit tasted plain and less sweet but looked so lush. Sanitary towels were affordable and less shameful to buy. I had to learn to assemble flat packs for my room which drove me insane. I did not have the patience and diligence of following instructions – where now, it is natural.

I thought I needed to secure some work urgently to be able to purchase a cheap car that will get me from one point to the other.

Over the next months, I would embark on walking to the university which was about a kilometre from my brother's home. I had to utilise the library to write a new resume then drive with my brother and drop these in different workplaces, several motels, aged care facilities and any cleaning or places requiring kitchen hand. I was called for interviews for two aged care facilitates and offered positions to start working just a few weeks of being in Australia before the semester started.

Mike was happy because he didn't have to pay for my tuition fees once I got a job. Being a senior lecturer, he had seen several international students that arrived and had to be deported due to various reasons for several years. It was hard to adjust to a very fast-paced environment with endless paperwork that I had never seen before.

I wondered where people stored so much paperwork in their homes. I was lucky to have learned English back at school; it was very easy to communicate, except the accent was a bit different from what I'd heard before. I had previously heard of British and American accents, not Australian. I got used to hearing, *"G'day mate"* and so many other shortened words and slang that I continue to learn. I enjoyed studying, and diving into the knowledge I so desired for many years.

Life got busy, especially when the semester started. I was required to attend classes full-time as an international student. I thought it was a lot of work but kick-starting the semester meant my journey had started for my learning. It meant getting closer to graduation to acquire better work for freedom from poverty. I had to fund myself fully through nursing home jobs. I had to pay for my textbooks, health care insurance and other costs here and there. I found it hard to navigate the fee structure undertaking four courses per semester, for international students because we had to clear the fee within the semester...

I thought perhaps offering some form of loans to students would have helped to ease the big rush and pressure, so they can immerse themselves in knowledge rather than just studying to pass the exams. I could see why some of the international students fail the courses or quit and go back home.

I had to attend hospital placements during the term which required spending days at the hospital without pay, and then going to work on my paid jobs at night which I found tiring but catered for my financial needs.

Placement days were challenging because it meant that I would be studying, writing assignments, and a full day of placement on top of working at night. I worked hard in understanding the human body, but I also thought it was fun during my placements to see all the education come alive in practice.

I knew I was not supposed to just enjoy the education; there was a requirement to pass all the courses and I did that. As an international student, you cannot afford to fail a course because it is expensive. Whatever it took me, I did not want to muck around. I wanted to get it done and dusted. I would take some textbooks to work where I could study if we got a small break, while other nights were a little busy and I could not get a chance.

Working in aged care facilities was a daunting experience for me – especially having to tend to an adult, showering them and attending to their personal needs. I felt challenged at first because it was wrong to look at or touch an adult in my culture. These are some of the fixed mindsets that I had to change and adjust to the awareness and expectations of being a nurse in this country.

I imagine that it is presumed that all students going through university and everyone who works in health care will adjust to such confronting scenes. But when it came to caring, I do not think people could access such anywhere or any other way and machines would not give them that. I was very confused at first seeing so many older people in the nursing home and wondered where their children were.

It was a big eye-opener in culture change and expectations for me here.

UNIVERSITY

In Kenya, especially my village, elderly and sick parents are cared for at home by their children unless they become critically ill when they go to the hospital. I have only witnessed them caring for themselves with small support encouraging the preservation of their dignity until they depart us. I wondered why Australians found it easy to place their loved ones in an aged care facility if they were capable of living at home with a bit of support.

It broke my heart a bit, although I came to understand later that some parents needed to be there for ongoing care and protection which was reassuring. I did say to myself that I would care for them as if they were my parents, as I can only imagine what they have gone through building this country and raising their children. I made sure every resident that I attended to felt cared for – not in a rush like just a worker, but as a person who placed the importance of personal care, values and thoughts as my priority. Like how I would feel if this was my mum and how I would like her to be cared for in my absence.

Most residents knew me by my name and were also intrigued by my journey and what I was doing in Australia. They encouraged me to go ahead and achieve my goals of becoming a nurse and building the women's shelter that I hoped to. That is how I related to them as my parents.

Being brought up in a deep tradition with extended family placed an important future role as a person. I learnt caring, respect, and treating others as I would like to be treated. It was a pleasure working with these old folks; they made a lot of jokes and taught me numerous Australian phrases and old songs like "Waltzing Matilda" and "Kookaburra Sits in the Old Gum Tree". They were a delight to look after, so full of life on good days. Some would give me candies from their jars. One even introduced me to liquorice that

I had never seen or tasted before! I remember thinking to myself, what on earth is that taste? Nowadays, you'll find them in my fridge!

University days went quickly due to the busy nature of the program and working between studies. I graduated, and I was able to find a job as a registered nurse and found a shared accommodation. I even purchased my first car, an old Holden Barina that made travelling easier and becoming completely independent. Night shifts took a big toil and it was difficult because I stopped eating well, resulting in extreme fatigue. When I secured a GP, I was found to be anaemic and had to start iron supplements that I was not taking religiously.

I came to learn that Australia is full of opportunities for people who are self-driven to study. Finding and pursuing courses is easy in multiple universities and colleges depending on your age and the level you want to start at. There is also transparency in acquiring your qualifications and securing a job in future, to reinforce my earlier imaginations and aspirations, depending on the path one wants to take, opportunities are open.

Further, you might be eligible to acquire scholarships or government loans if you are a citizen that requires you to start earning a certain amount of money to pay back the loan. I have utilised this service to acquire my master's degree from the University of Queensland and graduated in 2019, juggling two boys both under five and a full-time job.

I am now able to look back in gratitude thankful for the opportunity to have been able to pursue my dream. Sometimes it just takes persistence and tenacity to get there – it's what kept me going. I think that sometimes small steps can be achieved with patience and determination. It is tough at times and some challenges are hard to persevere, but if I did not try other ways of acquiring my degree

UNIVERSITY

when I failed to secure admission after high school, then it would be history. But because it pained me to miss that opportunity, I had to go through the hard way starting from NYS just because I wanted this so bad.

If I wanted a quick fix, I would not have attained my dream. This is only one example of how life can throw hard rocks at you; just keep dodging them by doing the work to get where you want to be irrespective of the timeline. Although it's a tough gig, nothing in this life comes easy and tough people do last.

Life requires one to take risks and persevere one loss after another, with the awareness that no matter the hardships in life, if you do not give up, you will get there.

Chapter Fourteen

MY BOYS

I met my ex-husband on the dancefloor on a Saturday night, at around 3am. My university friends and I had gone out following our graduation ceremony earlier in the day to celebrate our achievements. Later after dating for two years with a few consecutive dances and dressing up for the Melbourne Cup races, we decided to get married in Keppel Sands, just off Yeppoon Beach in North Queensland.

It was a simple but beautiful wedding with a few friends and family. After the wedding, we drove approximately seven hours to our honeymoon in East Bedarra Island Retreat and stayed there for a week. It was magical. We decided to have a honeymoon in Australia because I was already expecting our first son, Oliver. The only thing I wished for was for Mum to be able to attend, but due to many reasons, she was not able to, but she was happy for us.

LOOKING BACK TO MOVE FORWARD

Oliver was born six months after our wedding and three years later, his brother Jabari was born. After seven years of marriage, we agreed to part ways, but we have continued to work in harmony to support our boys.

As an immigrant, I worked through both my pregnancies. I must say, they were not too bad. I was lucky. Oliver arrived five weeks early at 35 weeks to share his birthday with his great-aunt on his dad's side. Oliver was tiny but a determined individual. I worked the whole week, then on Saturday I had the in-laws over during the day. Later, after they all left, my water kindly broke after dinner. No bag was packed, and I was alone at home when I felt something pop like a bubble. I felt warm water trickling down my leg.

No one prepares enough for the arrival of their first baby, regardless of all the classes and books. I called the ambulance which took me to Rockhampton Base Hospital and after 24 hours of bed rest and antibiotics to keep him in, the contractions set in and Oliver was born after two hours of labour. I did not have many faces in the birthing suite other than one midwife and a male student standing at the exit sign. I stuck with no pain medications for both births – even during a contraction episode. I knew that motherhood had set in when I had to forcefully nurse Oliver after I was warned that if he didn't latch one last time, the nurse would have to commence nasal gastric tube feed which made me feel sick at the time. He was a clever boy, and he might have heard the threat, so he latched on with some persistence and was left alone to feed naturally.

He has continued to be a tenacious and persistent but a great boy full of life and kindness. His teacher sometimes calls him her snuggle bunny!

For my second baby, Jabari, I worked until I went to my 37th week check. The doctor's check-up did not go as planned. Instead of returning home as I had expected, I was allowed to go home to pack some clothes and personal items and return to the hospital within the hour to be admitted. I had developed Cholestasis with three weeks left to go.

When I returned to the hospital, I was induced and a day later, Jabari was born after two hours of labour on our wedding anniversary. He has been the most caring child who is gritty and competitive since he realised that he has an elder brother to keep up with. They are both incredible and I love them so much.

I look at Oliver and wonder how fast time has passed, getting so tall yet skinny, calling himself a *"stickman"* and so fussy with his food. Oliver is kind and somewhat has the exact facial structure as his Mum which reminds me of how I was at his age. He has a forehead of a Kenyan.

LOOKING BACK TO MOVE FORWARD

He is a good runner and likes to participate in charity fun runs with me which is very impressive. He does not tire easily, but he can get a temper like his uncle at times, but we are working on that and learning to share with his brother.

Oliver is smart, he would like to be a scientist, but he likes to do less work and take the easy way. I am not supposed to say the word *'homework'* – it's forbidden, and we call it something else. I don't blame him, but I cannot just let it go without modelling an understanding. Otherwise, the learning context will be shoved out of the window to adopt *YouTube* and *TikTok* as he would wish. He likes to follow game rules and if you don't, you might be called a name, but I have reminded him that a colourful language is not welcome around our home or else we will wash his mouth with soap. He has kept the decency to some extent.

Jabari is very kind and nice to strangers; however, he is still learning to be nice to his elder brother, whom he likes to compete with. I call him a strong tiger in our family. He tries his food before he decides to eat it or not, which I think is brilliant because he makes up for his fussy brother and I am proud of him. I keep reminding them that I did not have a choice when growing up, but Oliver might quickly interrupt and say, *"But, we live in Australia, Mum!"*

I keep reminding them not to lose themselves, and that they could turn into brilliant humans if we understand how to merge my cultural values and those of their dad's positively because they are growing up in Western culture with no extended family around. They have not seen the hardships I talk about; it is utterly tricky to communicate my point, but we are getting there slowly.

I took Oliver to Kenya in 2015 then I returned with both in 2018 for a month and we all enjoyed it. Jabari would have been just two and a half, while Oliver was four and a half. They had a ball, running up and down Mathiga Hill chasing chickens and throwing rocks. They had endless diarrhoea accidents and never passed a single solid stool in the latrine for the first two weeks. Looking at their faces with all their bodies covered in red dirt; they both looked golden!

I was not concerned because I felt that they needed to experience this and build immunity for next time we visit, although my mum was concerned.

After two weeks, they got used to it and it settled; they had fun playing with their cousins. We even went to church and attended some traditional ceremonies where some of my nephews had undergone circumcision ceremonies. We explored our local markets and went to the creeks that I swam in as a child. We made different toys from dry wood and other recycled materials.

Each day spent at home was good, we didn't have a plan other than to take it easy and cook our favourite dishes like *chapatti* and the stews, *ugali* and *githeri*. It was fun. The only time we rushed around was the week when we had to travel to the Nairobi National Park for game drives. The animals were great to watch. We shared so much laughter and for me, I re-lived part of my childhood memories with my children and Mum, it was brilliant. I couldn't ask for more!

This time it was not so tough because I could afford to buy what we required, and this made life easier. It was beautiful, and the boys want to return, and it is on the cards.

There is no comparison of the privileges of what these children here have compared to their counterparts in my village. I like my boys to acknowledge and know that they are fortunate. Most children here are brought up encapsulated and almost treated as fragile as handling eggs. They blame their parents for their mistakes at school and fight with their peers, which should not be the case. Some children might mature out of this but others risk being stuck in this mindset of lacking resilience and introspection to live in this challenging world.

I remind them that we learnt negotiation skills through expressing ourselves in a safe way towards our peers with no blaming, hitting or being smart to each other. We had to accommodate each other and work as a team in all we did, considering the other person. Competition was minimal and only happened when it was a competition event or when it needed to happen. I observed that my children have limited negotiating skills and prefer to compete – very typical of siblings. Often, I sneak credit and encouragement when they stick to what we discussed and are nice to each other – although it does not last long enough for a triumph dance!

I had never imagined in detail what it was going to be like bringing up children of colour in Australia. I saw the schools and the education system where I thought how fantastic it is to have children and access all this free world-class education and opportunities. Although I was not all wrong, it has been tough some days, and other days fun, as they say *the joys of bringing up children*. For me, I would say the *challenges*, although I could not choose any other way if presented with the same opportunity of being a mother.

I adore them and have endless energy that keep me active. I said to myself that my children will never lack my love, and I will do my best to give them what I did not have. Basic needs, access to better health, good education. Then, they can do whatever they want because we live in Australia, as Oliver reminds me. The best place in the world with the best opportunities to build the life that you would wish. I will be there for them every step of the way.

Although we have hit some hurdles, it is not different from most families, and I try to look at the positive and the bigger picture. We compensate for hard days with short holidays and doing what they like.

When Oliver turned four, he started attending pre-kindy in Warwick, Queensland years ago. I must say that the trust was broken for one of his early school teachers. His brother was about to turn two and I was leaving them in one of the Good Start Early Learning Centres while I went to work and collecting them later in the evening. Most of the teachers there were great, but there was one teacher that physically assaulted Oliver.

After finishing work, I came to collect them. The teacher stopped me and said how Oliver was unsettled during the day. She did not mention the details and when I asked further, she just dismissed the details and went on a tangent of our conversation. I collected the boys, and we went home where I cooked them pasta bolognese – their favourite at the time. Oliver would squirm in pain every time he swallowed his food and eventually refused to eat anymore, saying that his throat was very sore. I asked him to open his mouth, so I could have a good look, and when he did, I couldn't believe what I saw. There were scratch marks and raw skin tears on the top back of his mouth.

When I asked Oliver what had happened, he told me that they were sitting on the floor listening to the teacher, who we'll call Diiba, then he talked to another child when they were supposed to be quiet. Diiba walked towards him and told him to shut up, when Oliver talked again, she walked back angrily, and told him to open his mouth.

She said to him this is the mouth that is talking, sticking her four fingers in, she added, *"You need to shut up."*

LOOKING BACK TO MOVE FORWARD

When I followed up with the centre, I was told that it was, *"Oliver's word against Diiba's"* and could not be substantiated. She said Oliver was choking off an apple and she was trying to save him – which was not true because Oliver would have said so.

Why didn't she mention it to me when we met at the gate?

It was also confirmed later by another teacher who left the centre that this lady tends to hurt children, and nothing gets done. I later got a call from her police friend threatening me, saying I needed to keep quiet and leave it at that, he said he would take the case himself. I wondered why such people exist in a community, importantly looking after vulnerable people. If this or similar incidents have happened to other children, why has nothing been done?

Sadly, Oliver continues to talk about this unpleasant incident to this day.

It pained me, and I don't think any parent wants such an outcome and trauma for their child caused by people who are entrusted with their care.

Chapter Fifteen

RACISM

There is enough ongoing awareness about racism and its forms but not enough to make racists wake up themselves. No one deserves to be treated unfairly regardless of where they come from, their skin colour, identity, their status or even their disability.

Racism is so ingrained in Australia and I have been a victim of it. I wish to also say that I have encountered many beautiful Australian people and friends who are genuine, and I wish to separate them from generalisation because they have embraced the diversity.

LOOKING BACK TO MOVE FORWARD

Years ago, I worked with this top immigrant female doctor of colour who said to me, *"Lillian, you will always be discriminated against because you are black."* She advised that she had also found it hard when she migrated. Now, she can talk back to racists when they throw racist comments or acts towards her as she has grounds.

Like most countries, you find a section of people who can't fathom what you are doing in their country or will straight up ask you, *"What made you come here?"* – yes, for real, in this century. These questions can be genuine but if you are culturally aware, you can pick on those who want to be pricks.

I have seen qualified immigrants getting replaced by unqualified/inexperienced white people and wondered if the bosses who do such acts sleep well at night feeling accomplished. They do not attend professional development or do objective supervision to reflect on their practices because they do not get questioned and simply don't get it.

Most Australians have cognisance of what an overseas person brings here, whether they come by boat or plane. They go out there and work on farms or hard labour that is uncompromised.

Most immigrants working in big companies or health care centres go extra mile to acquire post graduate studies to qualify because they want to set a competitive distance to put them ahead when looking for a job. Most of them have undertaken self-education to attain their qualifications which sometimes never comes easily with some people having the heartache of studying English in their adult life before acquiring other qualifications.

Immigrants bring with them a wealth of knowledge, hard work, dedication, and teamwork, with a lot of love in their hearts to give to Australian people and those from overseas equally. They feel bad to say no when called to fill a shift on weekends, overtime and public holidays when most of their Australian counterparts continue to say, *"Don't overwork, look after your health."*

They do this to support their families who live here and relatives overseas. As a manager hiring, if you find yourself looking for other unprofessional reasons other than merits to not give a candidate of colour some work while you offer it to their white counterparts with less qualifications, experience and merits, then you are racist. You need cognisance because people may not approach you directly to explain how a racist looks or feels inside.

I want to stress that as a Kenyan immigrant, most people in my situation are very busy. They do not have family or friends from primary school or cousins living here in Australia. I have friends back home, and I have made a few genuine friends and colleagues that I can count on. Immigrants strive hard to find those genuine people who are authentic and intuitive to form lasting and trusting friendships. Their mood does not fluctuate every day whether they are having a tough day or not, they are consistent.

In the past, I have found some known people to be superficial and cared to compare themselves with others wondering how one can be here for a few years and attain a degree, or master's and have purchased a home or two or acquired this and that. These are the few people who have made some of the immigrants' experiences in Australia awful.

I wish to separate those who are racially aware and have genuinely embraced everyone as equal and recognise hard work, unless proven otherwise. It might be okay if it is something you can shake off and move on without disrupting your life or that of your children, but if this is the opposite, then you wonder how that keeps on happening in Australia due to being of a different skin colour.

It is sad at work when you encounter some rotten minds full of nepotism, favouritism, bullying and corruption entrenched in some Australian health facilities while staff who question get intimidated. Luckily, I have grown and kept looking at these treatments through a different lens, embracing them as part of my journey. I trust easily which is okay, but recently after I turned 40, I started realising that you need to choose carefully whom to trust and whom you put in which basket.

Once you have an experience that shakes you, it is important to draw attention to it in a positive way and dig deeper, and you will grow from it. If you are happy enough to keep walking through your journey with or without some people, then keep doing exactly that.

On a positive note in light of some of the Australian health systems, I must say that we have a great health care system, and I am privileged to live in Australia. I wish to separate people with bad behaviour from others who give their absolute best with hope for the best outcome in all they do.

Recently I was riding a dirt bike in a friend's paddock interstate – in New South Wales, over the school holidays with my boys. I had an accident that saw my index finger lodged in the chain dismantling the top joint, and the thumb was cut across the top joint to near amputation.

After a two-hour ride on the ambulance to Cobar Hospital and getting flown three hours by air ambulance to Westmead Hospital, NSW trauma unit, the plastic surgeons worked tirelessly for six hours in the theatre. They completely vascularised my thumb and did a bone graft to my index finger instead of chopping them off!

RACISM

After two weeks in the hospital, the fingers have healed extremely well and are still on a journey to an amazing outcome. Thanks to the team at the Westmead hospital who did their absolute best to get my fingers as best as they could.

On my journey, I learnt that respect is a two-way traffic and immigrants demand respect back that they give, to live together in harmony. They do not need pity or favouritism; they just need fairgrounds of transparency that are safe and accommodating of everyone and recognition of everyone's efforts and good intentions.

As an immigrant at work, I don't know how many times I have defended myself to prove my worth even though I know I do my best enough. I reported an issue to a director once from an outright bully and I was shocked he couldn't face this bully to ask to sit and talk about the issue. He asked if I had forgiven the person and moved on. I replied that I did forgive, but not forgotten, and not going to trust them again. Then he said to me, *"Unfortunately, you must learn to work with her as she can't change her habit. We must work and deal with such people."*

I was shocked because I thought he would suggest mediation. I thought to myself, *"Thank you; she has been empowered to keep dishing it out to people who do not deserve it, with no consequences."* She was fuelled to never change.

We don't need unnecessary stress from unhappy person who wants to cause trouble to other people due to their lack of introspection.

I don't think people have time for such rubbish because they already have a lot going on in their lives. How do we treat people as they deserve, and who administers justice for those wronged unjustly?

LOOKING BACK TO MOVE FORWARD

Importantly, how do we spread a message of kindness to everyone who needs to hear it?

We should all reflect and be responsible for our actions towards others.

Ask about each one's day with genuine curiosity, their path, and how they view life because it is a precious gift to be living in this beautiful country. Instead of getting caught up with jealousy and hate that we don't need on this planet. Hate brews war; let us reflect, brew peace and accommodate each other.

We need to be insightful in all we do because we must co-exist. No one is untouchable by life struggles – whether it is us, our parents, children, grieving, or supporting a friend going through a rough patch.

For me, I will do my bit in making the world a better place. I will support anyone I come across because I have awareness. What about you?

What can you do in your ability to help change the world?

Don't we all wish to have a life free of heartaches?

Chapter Sixteen

REFLECTION

Healing comes when we learn to process all our life experiences in gratitude.

I am grateful for the person I am today, knowing that my life has not been easy, but I refused to give up. We own the stories we tell, let us tell stories that will encourage and uplift others, and let us not dig a hole in someone's heart due to our behaviours and words that do not reflect how we physically present outright.

I have seen people quit work, move to different locations, and go completely crazy due to the consequence of being gaslighted by friends or colleagues they trusted. There is nothing wrong with positive criticism but when the goal is to hurt the other, it is unethical. Ensure that you choose where you get your feedback from because not everyone is happy with your progress, you are wise

LOOKING BACK TO MOVE FORWARD

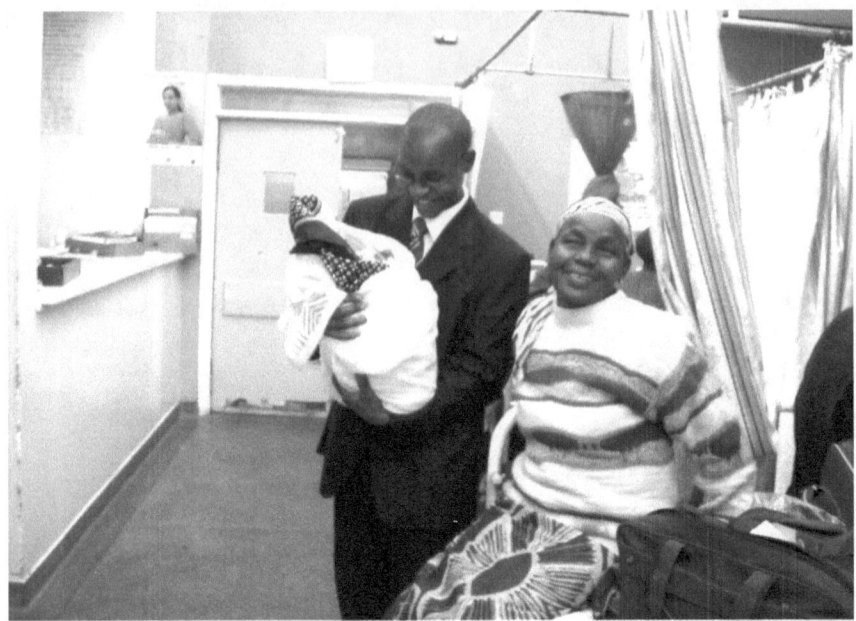

enough to know that. At the end of the day, you are the ultimate decision-maker in your life.

My advice is to talk to a friend or a trusted colleague who knows you better, as opposed to doubting yourself. I found that if you make room in your brain for self-doubt, you will believe it. If you clear your head and know your self-worth and can get through a rough patch, your brain works hard to keep focused on avoiding the sinkhole. Just hold on to something that makes you feel better. Go ahead and tell yourself that you are enough.

It is not you – it is them. You are more than enough irrespective of the rough patch because these are tests in our lives that come and go like a dark cloud. Think of it in the context that you are an ocean that doesn't run dry; you have abundance.

Remind yourself that even the ocean gets the waves that come and go, meandering through still rocks on the bottom, to the sand

REFLECTION

and the banks in harmony, the waves do not change the ocean. Instead, they make the ocean agile and dance. That is my theory and I like to look at the ocean and imagine that is me. So much of everything in abundance, including shells, sand, animals, and creatures – you name it. The patches we go through in life create diversity and abundance. The wisdom and the lessons we learnt did not come easy but with the years of encountering, embracing and learning from every single bump that stopped us and made us toss and turn at night. Even though the ocean has deeper and shallow ends, and gets rough waves when it storms, it is part of existence that we must trust and embrace to learn to rise from the bottom.

We can be so hard on ourselves and work hard to transform, to fit in or be who others want us to be, but I believe that we all have the very best version of ourselves that we truly feel connected to.

Be happy with who you are. It is only then that we realise our true worth. I desire to look back one day and see myself as an old woman full of zest, having given it all that I could and having contributed towards positively changing someone's life. I am motivated to inspire another child, a woman or a man to not give up regardless of their tough journey in life.

All I know is that I am very tough, in my skin, heart, mind, drive and desire to keep going and not into competing with anyone because I am in my own journey, and so is everyone else. I explore positives in all situations and get filled with joy when I hear a success story.

I am a liberal yearning for change, and I seek understanding; I avoid causing trouble and I embrace *my* kind of people that I meet on my journey.

LOOKING BACK TO MOVE FORWARD

I have been told that, *"Lilly, we all love working with you. I have never heard you say no to anyone ever. You do your best, you are a great colleague, and there is nothing wrong with your work."*

My former clients have said, *"I miss hearing from you, you changed my life. Please don't change what you do."*

I believe it is not just the voice; it is what comes out of my voice. In genuine recognition and holistic acknowledgement of their struggle, their success and accomplishments. I am brought up to believe that life is not an open book, but we can all find more when we keep turning the pages. This is a page of my history that I hope will inspire someone. Let's all try our best and cultivate such awareness and understanding.

My urge is to do something for you and others that makes you feel happy in your heart.

As a woman from a small village, I am proud to be where I am at my own self today. Without material but wisdom to spread that we all can make a difference in others' lives in a positive way. I am also living miles away from my mother. That means I am not only a mother to my children, but I must be my own mother, right here and now trusting myself to take the right direction in life.

Although rocked, I did not wither. My insecurities and anxiety within me, when they surge, I remember my upbringing and continue to see past bad days. I dive down there, remembering the values that guide me.

I often say to my children that they must keep walking, running, and sprinting like Kenyan warriors. We laugh and think it is funny but for me, it is the reality. When they grow up, they will understand

REFLECTION

and appreciate the importance of staying focused and not giving up. To keep their head up, especially when one of Oliver's classmates says to him, *"You are black, and your skin looks like a poo colour."*

As a mother, when your child says that to you, it feels helpless that you are not there to protect them from such bullies. How do I guide them without scaring them that although the world can be filled with cruelty, they are loved, worthy and they must keep strong?

I like to remind them that in a race, Kenyans never give up. They pace the race and run behind their competitors until the end, then sprint to finish. I encourage them to have some grit and inspiration to navigate this part of the world, in our colour. Because we cannot cover it, we speak about it so that we know how to appreciate ourselves and learn what to expect and how to deal with it in a way that does not break us, but through ways that shape us into better humans.

I teach them that we do not choose what we encounter, but we have a choice of dealing with the encounter, not through fighting, but through wisdom in how we handle conflicts with our peers and move on. By discovering a positive from a negative experience.

When I look back ten years ago and the experiences that have passed, it comforts me to know that any painful experience you are going through now will pass. If you embrace that, you will know that you cannot change what has happened, but you hold the wheel to your life to steer in the direction that suits you.

Try to live and laugh, put the hurts back, and if memories surface, acknowledge them because they are part of you now. I often say to myself that I can't walk from Kenya to Australia and have just one story!

LOOKING BACK TO MOVE FORWARD

Keep throwing them to me, and I will get up and keep going, I do not quit because I do not know any different.

As we all know, everyone experiences a hurdle on their journey. If you haven't experienced a hurt or burden that requires you to have a sleepless night, then you haven't lived!

When I look back at my young self, I would change only one thing, and that's having a meal each day when I was a child, because I was always hungry… I remember a few times when I thought I was full enough. But then we made it, with persistence, resilience and grit, now, I have a choice of the food I would like to eat. And that is something I do not take for granted.

To you, my beautiful reader, my name means journey in my mother tongue (*Kagendo*); a long journey. I have come to believe that part of my journey is discovering what has been good for me and cherishing milestones with gratitude. I remind you to do the same and believe it will work for you because it continues to work for me.

Breaking moments strengthen me by building an extra pillar to support myself to keep going. I have lived a good life to where I am at present, keeping all the positives with a smile.

I acknowledge that at times life handed me both rotten and great gifts, but I wish to leave those bad ones behind, consolidate and cherish my great feeling right now, having healed and grown.

To have this feeling, I have had to recognise how far I have come, acknowledging that all parts of my life belonged to me whether stressful or peaceful and exuberant.

REFLECTION

Gratitude did not force me to be happy while my heart was broken, unsettled and chaotic.

Instead, gratitude bore forgiveness and self-compassion that helped repair the broken bonds from my childhood through to adult life reminding me who I am. It also helped to free the heavy burden of hate, regrets and condemnation to make way for a lighter feeling of peace and love.

I honour the lessons and wisdom from my experiences with no doubts that many other people have gone through worse circumstances and have come out the other side as stronger, better humans and able to help others past their hurdles. I gift you this feeling, to look back to your experiences, I encourage you to embrace them and move on, at your own pace.

Looking back, some people would say that my experiences were traumatic. Indeed, in some sense, it can be argued to be traumatic. You can stand in the middle and call it anything you feel like because everyone has a story in their life that has been traumatic in their own way. Someone else may think that it is what makes us unique.

I will go with the latter because what I made from my experiences is what got me here to share it, to say to you that whatever experience you have gone through or are experiencing right now, never give up, dig deep and find some strength, it will pass.

Everyone has their own experiences. Embrace yours and live well.

Some may be keen to share, while others are not ready to visit there yet, to open that lid. It is okay to give yourself the time that you need to be ready to set yourself free.

LOOKING BACK TO MOVE FORWARD

As I open my lid, I wish to leave mine here, to feel free. To consolidate.

My hope is that I have inspired you, and when you are ready to open yours, you will know.

Embrace others and be kind.

Love and light.

REFERENCES

Action urged on teenage pregnancy and HIV, as a new report reveals high rates in Homa Bay. (unicef.org, https://tinyurl.com/yckh9mwz)

INFORMATION ABOUT KARIBU WOMENS AND CHILDRENS HOME

Soon, I hope to build a women's and children's shelter in my community back in Kenya. Karibu will be built on a two-acre land that I purchased over the last few years while living in Australia, located three kilometres away from my home.

The name, *'Karibu'*, is a Swahili word that means 'welcome'. The shelter will welcome women and children seeking safety and security to operate confidentially to protect them until they are ready to move out in their own time.

It will be run by volunteers for a start, but I hope to have trained staff in the fields of nursing and medicine, pathology, teachers and other areas of trade to train and empower women and young people to be independent.

LOOKING BACK TO MOVE FORWARD

During the time of their stay, needs will be identified, and support will be offered accordingly. They will have health checks and medicine, a safe bed, shower, food, personal items and safety. There will be trade offered and workshops to train the residents on a need basis.

I plan to travel back and forth to supervise this project until completion. This initiative would change the lives of many people and I urge you to be curious about how you can get involved. We will need water, mattresses, food, shoes, and anything you no longer need in your house.

If you would like to consider a monthly tax-deductible donation, this will go towards changing a woman and a child's life for good. Please get in touch with me on the details below if you have questions about how the shelter will operate and if you would like to donate or volunteer once completed.

Lillian Muchiri
Website: Lillianmuchiri.com.au
Email: lillianmuchiri@yahoo.co.uk
Facebook: https://facebook.com/lillianmuchiri
*Instagram: @lillianmuchiri_*
Twitter: @lillianmuchiri1

ABOUT THE AUTHOR

Born on the 1st of January sometime between 1979-1982 (no one has ever been able to tell her what year she was born) as her mum walked to the hospital, Lillian Muchiri was named Kagendo, meaning *'journey'* in her mother tongue. Lillian grew up in a polygamous family in a remote village called Mathiga Marimanti in eastern Kenya.

Growing up, Lillian and her siblings did not see any clean water they used to fetch water from a creek and caves and would carry it on their backs. Girls were required to look after their siblings. They were uneducated, beaten up, faced FGM without a choice and had nowhere to escape to. Lillian embraced these traditions as normal practices of growing up.

With maturity and worldly knowledge, Lillian realised that these practices were unjust and unfair. She vowed to her mother that she would take up a cause to challenge these traditional customs and she needed to be brave to deliver change and hope for Kenyan women.

LOOKING BACK TO MOVE FORWARD

At age 26, Lillian moved to Australia where she embraced the new cultural differences and awareness. She undertook a Nursing Degree at the Central Queensland University and later completed Master of Nursing at University of Queensland. For the past few years, she has been working as a Clinical Nurse which she enjoys and feels that it is her passion to bring awareness and educate people and society about issues that continue to impact people in many communities

Recently, she has embraced a role of a motivational speaker, mentor, life and a recovery coach. She enjoys working with and inspires people to get their lives back after a difficult patch.

Lillian hopes to inspire the young generation by creating awareness of what children these days take for granted, forgetting how hard their parents and those of previous generations worked tirelessly for them to access and live comfortably. Lillian hopes to help transform the community where she grew up to give back and change the future generation, shining light to enforce nurturing of every woman and child to live in harmony.

Lillian is also desperate to highlight male leaders who need to change repetitive patterns and learn from female leaders to move forward. Her hope is for a change in some of the cultural taboos while keeping the traditions alive in an evolving and educative way.

She currently loves living on the beautiful Sunshine Coast of Queensland, Australia with her two beautiful boys.

LILLIAN MUCHIRI

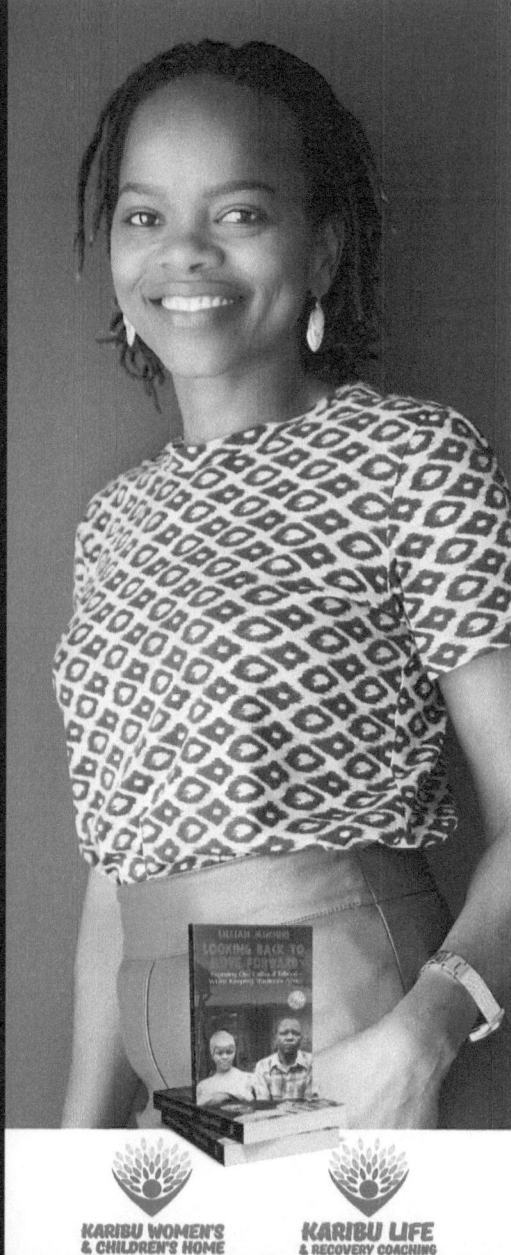

Lillian Muchiri is the bestselling author of *Looking Back to Move Forward*.

She is an intuitive, conscious, motivating speaker who reflects on her upbringing and the grit that saw her move from Kenya to Australia, embracing a new cultural awareness that differed from what she had grown up with and thought was normal.

For the last decade, Lillian has been working as a Clinical Nurse in various disciplines. In the recent past, Lillian has been specialising in the mental health field where she has helped many people recover from mental health and life challenges and reclaim their lives.

Lillian runs Karibu Life & Recovery Coaching, where she works with clients from diverse backgrounds. She works with immigrants, NDIS clients, LGBTQIA+ and all success-minded individuals to build on their strengths to overcome any life challenges, reclaim their lives to become independent and move forward.

Lillian has been connecting with male elders and leaders in her village back in Kenya to instil an awareness of the plight of children and women in Kenya. She has been sharing her experiences to encourage introspection and the nurturing of every child and woman to reach their potential.

She easily connects with the young generation and anyone seeking advice about career opportunities and choices. She inspires them to appreciate and embrace what the older generations have worked hard for so that they can enjoy the life they have now.

Lillian's signature talks are:

- Getting unstuck from emptiness, relationships, career advice and encouragement, bullying and workplace issues.
- Overcoming trauma, grief, and other mental health illnesses.
- Addiction, and psychosocial adjustments.
- Courage, resilience & determination.

Lillian radiates a welcoming energy as she speaks about the life lessons that transformed and shaped her to be the person she is today, that can help other people find their niche to unleash their potential.

KARIBU WOMEN'S & CHILDREN'S HOME

KARIBU LIFE & RECOVERY COACHING

To engage Lillian to speak at your next event, you can contact her below:

✉ lillianmuchiri@yahoo.co.uk

 Lillian Muchiri   @Lillianmuchiri   Lillian Muchiri   @LillianMuchiri1

ACKNOWLEDGEMENTS

I am grateful to be able to jot down and share my experiences with the world, to you my beautiful reader, I gift you a feeling of healing, acceptance and moving on.

Thank you to my beautiful sons, Oliver and Jabari. You have continued to show your resilience. Your beautiful and caring nature is slowly emerging. Continue believing in yourselves.

To my siblings, my step-siblings and their families; thank you for trusting in our journey.

In my long journey, I found wonderful conscious and genuine friends who have always supported me and my children during hard times. If you have influenced me positively, then you are my gang. You know who you are, please accept my gratitude.

The team at Westmead Hospital Plastics, thank you so much for enabling me to finish writing my book by putting my fingers back together! They have healed well.

Lastly to my publishing team at Ultimate 48 Hour Author, thank you for making my publishing dream come true. I appreciate you all.

www.ingramcontent.com/pod-product-compliance
Lightning Source LLC
Chambersburg PA
CBHW030038100526
44590CB00011B/252